BARNES & NOBLE BASICS™

giving a
Presentation

by Jude Westerfield

Formerly published as
I need to give a Presentation, Now What?!

**BARNES
&NOBLE
BOOKS**

Other titles in the **Barnes & Noble Basics**™ series:
Barnes & Noble Basics *Using Your PC*
Barnes & Noble Basics *Wine*
Barnes & Noble Basics *In the Kitchen*
Barnes & Noble Basics *Getting in Shape*
Barnes & Noble Basics *Getting a Job*
Barnes & Noble Basics *Saving Money*
Barnes & Noble Basics *Using the Internet*
Barnes & Noble Basics *Retiring*
Barnes & Noble Basics *Using Your Digital Camera*
Barnes & Noble Basics *Getting Married*
Barnes & Noble Basics *Grilling*
Barnes & Noble Basics *Buying a House*
Barnes & Noble Basics *Volunteering*
Barnes & Noble Basics *Getting a Grant*
Barnes & Noble Basics *Getting into College*
Barnes & Noble Basics *Golf*

introduction

When Dave got the call from his boss asking him to give a
presentation on the new product line his team had developed, he
knew it was make it or break it time. "It was a strange mix
of excitement and sheer terror. I've always been leery of
public speaking. But now I was asked to talk about something I knew all about. I figured I could do that. But as I
sat down to work on my presentation, I was over-
whelmed with questions I realized I couldn't answer.
What should I say? What should I leave out? Should
I use PowerPoint or rely on handouts? How long
should I talk? What about questions and answers? What did I
really want to say? Why is this so hard?"

Why indeed? Most people blame fear of public speaking. Yes,
it's scary to talk before a group. But the real problem, as most public speaking pros will tell you, is lack of preparation. That's where
Barnes & Noble Basics *Giving a Presentation* comes in. It walks
you through the art and science of giving a rock-solid presentation.
All you need to know is here: choosing your topic, researching it,
writing it out, rehearsing, adding visuals, working on your voice,
and much more. Knowledge is power. So read on and learn how to
power up your presentation.

Barb Chintz
Editorial Director, the Barnes & Noble Basics™ series

table of contents

Chapter 1 **Getting over your fears** 6

You can do it! **8**   Evolution of a nervous wreck **10**   Rx for nerves **12**
Why be nervous, you're the expert **14**   How to lower the pressure **16**
Now what do I do? **18**

Chapter 2 **Thinking your talk out** 20

Know the purpose of your talk **22**   Making it fascinating **24**
Using humor **26**   Using quotations **28**   Making it better **30**
Where to go for facts **32**   Now what do I do? **34**

Chapter 3 **Writing your talk out** 36

Outline your talk **38**   Organize your points **40**   The basic outline **42**
A basic speech **44**   Writing for the ear **46**   Your opening **48**
The body of your talk **50**   Making it flow **52**   Revising your talk **53**
The wrap-up **54**   Handling a Q&A session **56**   Now what do I do? **58**

Chapter 4 **How to say it** 60

To read or not to read **62**   Notes for emphasis **64**   Your voice **66**
Your breathing **68**   Vocal tools **70**   Fixing common speech faults **72**
Rehearsing your speech **74**   Now what do I do? **76**

Chapter 5 **Appearances matter** 78

Your entrance **80**   Body language **82**   Eye contact **84**   Your personal
style **86**   Your dress **88**   Now what do I do? **90**

Chapter 6 **Types of talks** 92

Types of talks **94**   Informational talks **96**   Persuasive talks **98**
Motivational talks **100**   Introductions **102**   Panelist talks **104**
Being a Moderator **106**   Leading a seminar **108**   Now what do I do? **110**

Chapter 7 **Your audience** 112

Know thy audience **114**   What does your audience expect? **116**
Will they like your presentation? **118**   Will they be comfortable? **120**
What is your audience saying? **122**   Now what do I do? **124**

Chapter 8 **Using visuals** 126

The power of visual aids **128**   Setting the scene **130**   35mm slides **132**
Presentation software **134**   Videotape **136**   Overhead transparencies **138**
Flip charts **140**   Handouts **142**   Tools of the trade **144**
Now what do I do? **146**

Chapter 9 **PowerPoint power** 148

What is PowerPoint? **150**   Starting **152**   AutoContent
outlines **154**   Meet PowerPoint **156**   Editing presentations **158**
Using design templates **160**   Other PowerPoint features **162**
New views on your slides **164**   Transitions **166**
Build slides **168**   Using blank presentations **170**
Printing and presenting **172**   Tips for using slides **174**
Now what do I do? **176**

Chapter 10 **From start to finish** 178

You get "the call" **180**   Two weeks to go **182**   Ten days to go **184**
One week to go **186**   Five days to go **188**   One day to go **190**
The morning of your talk **191**   Ten minutes to go **192**
You're on! **193**   Almost over! **194**   Closing Statement **195**
Now what do I do? **196**

Glossary 198

Index 200

CHAPTER 1

Getting over your fears

You can do it!
Turn your anxieties into affirmations **8**

Evolution of a nervous wreck
How fear works in your body **10**

Rx for nerves
Turn your fear into empowering energy **12**

Why be nervous, you're the expert
Let your passion and knowledge show **14**

How to lower the pressure
Ten smart questions to ask first **16**

Now what do I do?
Answers to common questions **18**

If you panic at the thought of speaking before a group, you are not alone. In studies of human fears, public speaking consistently tops the list of things people fear most— ahead of flying, snakes, even death. As comedian Jerry Seinfeld points out, that means if you're at a funeral, you'd rather be in the casket than delivering the eulogy.

you can do it!

Seize this opportunity to stand out!

Chances are one of these days your boss is going to call you in to discuss a project you've been managing for the past few months. Maybe she'll suggest that you brief the executive committee on market trends and their long-term implications for the company. Being the pro that you are, you will appear enthusiastic, agreeable, even confident about the idea. But inside—deep inside—the primal "fight or flight" urge will kick in. Your pulse will quicken; your face will pale; your breathing will become shallow. The words "Why me?" will scream in your head and threaten to tumble out of your mouth, now frozen stiffly into a smile. "Of course I'll do it," you'll say, but deep inside you'll think, "I'll die up there."

Don't panic. Take a deep breath. You won't die up there. In fact, with the right attitude and preparation, you won't even remember why you were so scared in the first place.

The truth is, you've been selected to speak for a reason. You are the one with the right background, competence, and familiarity with the topic. Sure, there could be other reasons why you've been selected to hit the podium. Maybe your manager wants you to have exposure to the upper echelons of your organization. Or she may feel that you deserve recognition among your peers for your superb work. Whatever the reason, seize this opportunity to shine. Remember that you are uniquely qualified for your time in the spotlight. So turn "Why me?" into "Yes, me!"

TOP TEN BENEFITS OF
GIVING A PRESENTATION

- Gain recognition for your ideas.

- Improve your position in the company, industry, community.

- Win the admiration of your peers.

- Build your credibility among your audience.

- Set yourself apart from the others.

- Demonstrate your competence and uniqueness.

- Hone your leadership potential.

- Extend your sphere of influence.

- Earn the respect of your superiors.

- Develop confidence in yourself.

evolution of a nervous wreck

Our ancestors were afraid of tigers and bears; we're afraid of sales presentations

It's hard to imagine that all the dreaded physical effects of fear—sweaty palms, racing heart, shallow breathing—were originally designed to empower us against lunging tigers and bears. But that's how the "fight or flight" response works. At the first sign of a threat, your brain triggers the release of cortisol and adrenaline—powerful hormones that signal the alarm to either fight or flee. Here's what happens: Your pupils dilate so that you see better. Your blood pressure soars, shutting down tiny vessels near your skin so that you can sustain a surface wound without bleeding to death. Blood drains from the face, neck, and head and goes to those muscles that are needed for self-defense, such as your thigh muscles, so you can fight harder or run away faster.

But what happens if the threat is not an attacking bear, but just a little daydream you are having of speaking before an audience? Believe it or not, the adrenaline will pump just as hard regardless of whether the threat is imagined or real. And if that isn't bad enough, if you don't use up that adrenaline by physically fighting or fleeing, those pulsing hormones send little shock waves through your body, leaving you feeling exhausted. This is why nervous speakers who panic at the very thought of speaking end up giving a tired and shaky presentation. Don't fret. The good news is that your nervous energy can be converted into enthusiasm for your topic.

The fight or flight response can cause one more problem: haunting memories. When under acute stress, the brain infuses fearful emotions into the adrenaline mix to make the experience that much more vivid. This could explain why people who have had an unpleasant public speaking experience dread public speaking. Their memory is too filled with fear to make trying again an option. If you fit into this category, you are not alone. But don't let one bad speaking experience ruin your efforts. Let this book show you some inside tricks to outwit your scary memories.

YOU ARE NOT ALONE

If you panic at the thought of speaking before a group, you are not alone. In studies of human fears, public speaking consistently tops the list of things people fear most—ahead of snakes, flying, even death. As comedian Jerry Seinfeld points out, that means if you're at a funeral, you'd rather be in the casket than delivering the eulogy.

"I turn pale at the outset of a speech
and quake in every limb and in all my soul."
—Cicero, the great Roman orator and statesman

"The only difference between the professionals and the novices is that the pros have taught the butterflies to fly in formation."
—Edwin Newman, television commentator

"Stagefright is the sweat of perfection."
—Edward R. Murrow, broadcast journalist

"The human brain starts working the moment you are born and never stops until you stand up to speak in public."
—George Jessel, comedian

Rx for nerves

Harness your fear to work in your favor

Imagine this: You're at the podium. The room is dark except for a spotlight blanching your already ashen face. You can't quite make them out, but you know that there are people staring at you, waiting, expecting. You fumble with your notes. A little voice is shouting inside your head: "They're staring at me; I sound foolish; I'm not smart enough; I'm not making sense."

Sound familiar? Say hello to fear.

Now stop and take a deep breath and come back to reality. What went wrong in your imagined presentation? Something we all do: You lost your **focus**—the reason you are talking. The audience isn't there to see you (unless you're a famous movie star). They are there to hear the information you are about to share. So let go of the self-centered concerns and put your nervous energy into your talk. Make it relevant to your listeners and fun. If you connect with your topic, you and your topic will connect with the audience.

HIRING A SPEECH COACH

Speech coaches can help you polish your speaking style with tips and techniques that work for the pros. You can learn how to use your body language, better organize your presentation, manage your voice, control your nerves, and turn even the most hostile questions into opportunities to get your point across. Where do you find a speech coach? Check under "Public Speaking" in your Yellow Pages, or check with your company's communications department for a consultant recommendation.

The only thing to fear is fear itself

I was so nervous about having to give a speech to our new Board of Trustees that I couldn't sleep for worrying about it. My boss suggested I see a speech professional. She asked me to talk about the last time I gave a talk. It was back in college. I was so nervous I almost passed out while speaking. My speech teacher gently explained that my fear about speaking was compounded by what had happened in college. She got me to practice breathing techniques that helped calm me down. I also put a picture of my brand-new baby girl up with me by the podium when I was speaking. That picture reminded me that I was definitely not in college anymore.

Martha G., Little Rock, Arkansas

WHAT TO DO TO CALM DOWN

Arrive Early Get familiar with the room in which you'll be presenting, as well as the podium, lectern, A/V equipment, and seating arrangement.

Meet & Greet Shake hands and chat with people before the program begins. Familiarity breeds comfort.

Breathe Try deep, rhythmic breathing to the count of ten, in through your nose and out through your mouth. Yawning also brings oxygen into the lungs, relaxes your throat, and helps you breathe more slowly, more steadily.

Familiar Faces Keep a photo of your child or pet (whoever makes you smile) tucked into your pocket or taped to your script. Glance at it as needed.

Act "As If" Smile warmly, be enthusiastic and confident, as if you were actually feeling that way. You may surprise yourself when you do.

Rubber Band Wear one around your wrist. Snap it every time you find yourself thinking negatively or getting lost in your talk.

Eye-connect Seek out a couple of friendly faces and eye-connect with them during your talk. Or eye-connect with empty chairs or spots on the carpet.

Clock Check If you are scheduled to talk for 20 minutes beginning at 3 p.m., remember that no matter how nervous you are, your talk will be done by 3:21—a finite time that will come and go in a flash, and you can get on with your life.

why be nervous, you're the expert

Take ownership of your presentation!

Your knowledge and experience bought you the right to be called "expert." But it's your unique point of view that will add real value to your talk. Whether you volunteered—or were volunteered—to make this presentation, your perspective on the topic is what permits you to take ownership of it.

Having a firm grasp of your subject matter is certainly key. However, if you don't feel fully up to speed on your topic, you'll need to do some in-depth research posthaste. Depending on the subject of your talk, try doing some Internet searches for presentations on the same topic that offer valuable ideas you can borrow. Seek out best practices in your industry, new developments in the field, or innovative thinking on the topic.

Once you've mastered the information, master the art of how best to communicate it. More on how to do that in chapter 4. Remember, your audience will appreciate the information more if you make it relevant to them. Get them to want to listen to your point of view, because ultimately there's something in it for them. Engage the audience with direct questions; share personal experiences; put conviction behind your words. When you communicate your passion for the subject, you'll also be communicating your expertise.

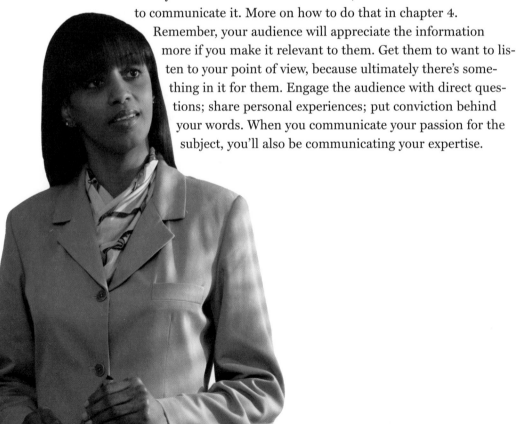

ASK THE EXPERTS

What steps can I take to make sure I am perceived as an expert?

The answer is simple: You will gain your audience's respect by the respect you show them. Be yourself. Be well prepared. Share your passion for your topic. Engage your audience with personal anecdotes or humor. Speak "with" your audience, not "at" them. Don't wear anything that draws attention away from what you are saying. Don't use grandiose words—keep your language clear, concise, and accessible. The example you set with your integrity as a speaker is the stuff of which leaders are made.

How do I communicate my expertise to the audience without sounding like I'm boasting?

The beauty of having someone else introduce you is that he or she can tell everyone how great you are! Even if you have to introduce yourself, be sure to tailor your introduction so that it focuses heavily on your experience in the topic you'll be presenting. Don't be shy here—play up your professional achievements, awards, and educational accomplishments. Your introduction can go a long way in establishing your credibility.

I have been asked to speak on a panel with four other experts. What do I do?

Being on a panel is a great way to begin your career as a public speaker. It lets you speak before the public, but because there are others speaking with you, the focus is not entirely on you. The panel should have a moderator whose job is to coordinate the talks of all of the speakers. Some moderators ask for notes in advance to make sure that the speakers don't talk about the same exact subject. If that is the case, then do so. Take advantage of any inside information your moderator may have about your audience. You want to know how many people you will be addressing and what specific information they are interested in. Also, inquire about the other speakers on your panel and what they will be speaking about. Ideally, you will want to meet your fellow panelists before you give your presentation. (For more information on speaking on a panel, see page 104.)

how to lower the pressure

The more information you have, the calmer you'll be

Before you start planning your presentation, you'll need to know some basic information to soothe your nerves. Here are the top ten questions you want answered before you say a word:

Who is your audience?

A simple question, but the answer speaks volumes. To make an impact with your speech, you'll want to tailor your talk to your audience. Even the most far-flung topics can be made relevant to niche groups. For example, if you are a scientist presenting the topic of global warming to a group of financial analysts, you might focus on the economic implications of your subject. If you are addressing coworkers, speak on familiar terms ("we" and "our") and include anecdotes that all employees will relate to. Always, always put your audience's interests first.

Why are they there?

You'll want to know the purpose of the gathering to help you tailor your speech. For example, if your talk is to provide key information, then consider using audiovisuals (see pages 126–145).

Is there a theme?

Very often, conferences and meetings will have an overall theme for the gathering, e.g., "The Millennium Outlook" or "Global Vision for Success." Find out what the theme is and weave it into your talk.

Who else is speaking?

If you are one of several speakers, find out the names of the other presenters and the titles of their talks. You may want to read up on their backgrounds to see how your speech topic can complement theirs.

How will the room be set up?

Find out how the audience will be arranged. Will they be sitting in rows or around tables? Will you be seated or standing when you speak? Is the room so large you will need a microphone?

What equipment will you have?

Having a lectern or podium will allow you to handle notes or a script easily. If you want to project slides, film, or a PowerPoint presentation, the room must be dark enough to enhance image quality and long enough to allow for a projector's lens to fill the screen.

How much time do you have?

Regardless of the amount of time you have to speak, structure your presentation so that you allow approximately 20% of the time you have to your opening, 70% to your major points, and 10% to your close. If you've been given more time than you need to present, use it for a Q&A at the end of your talk, or negotiate the timing issue with the meeting planner.

Where are you on the agenda?

Every good speaker thinks of his or her audience first. The time you are slated to speak will directly affect your audience's level of consciousness. If you speak before a coffee or lunch break, be sure not to run over your allotted time. In fact, you would be a hero for running short. If you are to speak during or after a cocktail reception, remember that your audience members may have had a few drinks and are probably not too receptive to an excessively technical or detailed speech.

Who is introducing you?

Find out who will introduce you, and be sure to thank that person by name when you get to the podium. If you would like your introducer to include specific points about your background, be sure to send a copy of your bio to the meeting planner well ahead of your speech.

What is the dress code for the event?

For a presenter, it is always better to err on the side of dressing up rather than down. This is doubly true if you are speaking to an "external" audience, that is, a gathering of people other than coworkers. If you are speaking to an "internal" audience of employees, your dress should be consistent with the standards of your company's dress code.

now what do I do?

Answers to common questions

I'm nervous now. Won't I be a wreck when it's time for me to speak?

You should expect to be nervous, but with good preparation you can communicate your nervousness as enthusiasm and passion for your topic. In fact, you should hope that you don't become overconfident! Too often, overconfident speakers lack animation in their delivery and don't establish a connection with their audience. Anxious speakers, however, usually get more comfortable once their talk is under way.

I am really short, and I'm afraid that I'll appear tiny at the podium and people will dismiss me as a lightweight. What can I do?

Two words here: Ruth Westheimer. When Dr. Ruth speaks to an auditorium full of people, the last thing they think about is how tiny she is. Her direct, engaging, and funny approach to her topic is what her audience remembers. The point here is that your presentation is not about you. Your audience is there to learn about your topic.

What if I don't feel qualified to give a talk?

Not feeling qualified may actually be your insecurity about public speaking coming through. One thing you should remember: No one in the audience has your unique perspective on the topic. Your ideas are your own, and this is your opportunity to be heard and respected.

A friend told me about the Dale Carnegie course in public speaking. Is that still around?

Yes, it is. There's a reason Dale Carnegie's public speaking programs are world renowned: They work. The Dale Carnegie system has grown into a global entity on one simple belief: that people have the power to reach their full potential. They offer three programs (Leadership Training for Managers, Sales Advantage, and the core public speaking program) that give people the tools to manage speaker anxiety while sharpening their communications and business skills. Classes and locations are available at **www.dalecarnegie.com**.

When should I start preparing for my talk?

As early as possible. Careful preparation leads to confidence and a successful presentation.

What if I make a mistake?

Everyone makes mistakes, and to do so from a podium only makes you human. The trick is how you deal with them. Don't draw attention to an error unless you have a humorous comeback. Above all, don't apologize for an honest mistake. For example, if you mispronounce a word or say words in the wrong order, simply stop and say what you were trying to say correctly and move on.

If I'm supposed to be connecting with my audience by making eye contact, how do I look at my notes?

One of the things you'll want to do in practice is to S-L-O-W down your delivery. Nerves can rev up your delivery to 78 rpm if you let them. You'll find as you slow down, you can glance ahead to your next point. Since you'll have done your practice sessions, you will easily be able to recall the point in full and deliver it fully and confidently while you focus on your audience instead of your notes.

NOW WHERE DO I GO?!

CONTACTS	PUBLICATIONS
The Speech or Communications Studies departments of many U.S. colleges and universities maintain Web sites that offer remarkably good tips about preparing and delivering effective presentations. The URLs are long, but they are worth the visit.	**The Complete Idiot's Guide to Public Speaking** by Laurie Rozakis
http://www.ukans.edu/cwis/units/coms2/vpa/vpa.htm	**7 Steps to Fearless Speaking** by Lilyan Wilder
http://www.personal.psu.edu/users/s/b/sbw3/workbook/	**How to Speak Like a Pro** by Leon Fletcher
http://www.wesleyan.edu/libr/tutlist.htm	**Inspire Any Audience** by Tony Jeary
http://www.ee.ed.ac.uk/~gerard/Management/art1.html	**How to Develop Self-Confidence and Influence People by Public Speaking** by Dale Carnegie
http://www.temple.edu/speech/	

CHAPTER 2

Thinking your talk out

Know the purpose of your talk
State your mission **22**

Making it fascinating
Use facts to bolster your presentation **24**

Using humor
The dos and don'ts of jokes **26**

Using quotations
Let other speakers help you out **28**

Making it better
Tips to brighten your presentation **30**

Where to go for facts
A treasure trove of books and Web sites **32**

Now what do I do?
Answers to common questions **34**

Think of a single-theme mission statement and let it guide the organization of your presentation. A one-theme mission will help you weed out information that is not essential to making your case.

know the purpose of your talk

Develop a mission statement before you start planning your talk

Too often, insecurity drives presenters to pack their talks with way too much data, charts, graphs, anecdotes, references, and statistics. If you find yourself piling on the factoids, keep in mind a saying that the Finnish people have, which goes, "The ship that sails by every wind never comes in the harbor." Just as ships lose their way by not plotting and sticking to one specific route, a speaker can be blown off course by covering too much in a presentation.

Before you begin planning your talk, ask yourself, "What is the one thing I want my audience to remember or do as a result of my speech?" The answer to this question is critical: It is the mission statement for your talk. Write it down and keep it in front of you as you begin thinking through what you want to say and how you want to say it. Remember that every point you make, every fact you include, every joke you tell should help you accomplish your mission. If it doesn't, delete it.

By narrowing your focus and pouring all your energy into accomplishing the one overriding goal of your talk, you will find it much easier to select the best information to help you build your case effectively and successfully.

ONE MISSION AT A TIME

Some people worry that if they limit their mission statement to one theme or objective they will run out of things to say. In fact, the opposite is true. Your audience has limited attention (as well as limited absorption—there's only so much information anyone can absorb). Using a single-theme mission statement to guide the organization of your presentation will help you weed out information that is not essential to making your case.

Sample Mission Statements

Your mission statement should sum up the one thing your audience should take away with them. Start with an action verb and build your mission around it. **I want my audience to:**

- **mobilize**

against construction of a waste treatment facility in our county

- **understand**

the history of public finance

- **appreciate**

the cultural contributions of African Americans

- **purchase**

at least 200 high-speed collating units

- **praise**

their children at least once a day

- **choose**

my travel agency for their business and personal needs

- **rally**

around the sales targets our company has set for the year

- **realize**

that excellent customer relations will improve our bottom line

- **seek**

professional tax-planning advice

making it fascinating

Create a picture with anecdotes, stats, and facts

Jay Brown, the chairman and CEO of MBIA, a major financial services firm, was about to address his employees. The company was in the middle of a difficult period, the first in its 25-year history. Though the company's balance sheet was very sound and the difficulty most certainly short-term, the chairman knew he had to convey to his employees that he understood their concern.

He began his talk this way: "This morning I was at the kitchen table, going through the bills and writing check after check over coffee. My 11-year-old daughter, Alex, sat down for her cereal and began watching me very intently. I finally asked her what she was

thinking about, and she looked up at me and asked, 'Dad, are we going broke?' After I assured her that our finances were quite safe, I began to realize that the insecurity she felt for that minute, as unfounded as it was, is a lot like what people here have been feeling over the last few weeks. I know it's been a very uncertain and challenging time for us, but I'm here today to tell you that our company's finances are indeed quite safe."

This chairman's very personal and real anecdote was an interesting parallel to his business situation. His story created an image that audience members could relate to, and because he told the story from his heart, he gained his employees' trust with his sincerity.

Anecdotes, statistics, and facts can be made unforgettable by presenting them in terms that your audience can visualize and internalize. For example, tell a real-life story your audience can relate to. Whatever you do, don't tell a story about the trials of writing your presentation.

STATISTICS THAT STICK

■ **Interpret your statistics for your audience:**
Following your recent advertising campaign, awareness of your company increased from 1.5% to 3% of the general public. Was the campaign a dismal failure or a great success? Your audience will understand that it was a success when you explain that awareness levels increased 100%.

■ **Give your stats a frame of reference:**
You are giving a talk on the inexact science of stock market predictions. You use the example: Wall Street analysts' predictions of high-tech stock earnings during early 1999 were wrong 44% of the time. But contrast this number with another: The average percentage of incorrect forecasts by amateur stock Web sites during the same time period was only 21%.

■ **Break your stats down for your audience:**
Instead of "$2 billion a year," say, "$5.5 million per day."

FABULOUS FACTS

■ **Expense accounts**
Paul Revere billed the Massachusetts State House 10 pounds and 4 shillings to cover his expenses for his ride.

■ **Change management**
The first edition of the book *The 100 Best Companies to Work for in America* was published in 1984. When the second edition rolled off the press in 1993, of the 100 companies cited in the original book, only 55 had survived.

■ **The value of a name or brand**
The Kwakiutl Indians of British Columbia pawn their names if they need money. Until the loan is repaid, the borrower is nameless.

using humor

You've no doubt heard the arguments against the use of humor in a speech: Jokes can alienate, offend, anger, confuse, or annoy an audience. While poorly delivered, inappropriate, or sarcastic jokes will backfire on you, be assured that the right joke can win your audience over from the get-go and may even be the only part of your speech they remember the next day.

Why is humor such a powerful influencer? A good joke will put your audience into a more relaxed and receptive mood. According to Stanford University studies, even one good belly laugh can boost mood-enhancing endorphins and melt muscle tension as effectively as ten minutes on a rowing machine. Additionally, humor has been shown to be a valuable component of leadership. A Temple University study found that people who use humor tend to wield more influence over group decisions.

Studies, of course, are important, but just ask yourself: Wouldn't you rather listen to someone who grabs your interest with a clever joke—who allows you to release a little tension and shows you it's safe to laugh in a business or formal setting? That's the person who will earn your attention and your trust. That's the person who scores a victory with every laugh.

A SK THE EXPERTS

I'd love to tell a joke during my talk, but how can I sound like a comedian?

First, don't try to sound like anyone but yourself. Enjoy yourself as you tell the joke, and your audience will follow suit. One tip from the great comics is that the best jokes use timing to build tension, which is then released through laughter. The more tension, the bigger the laugh.

HUMOR DOS

- Use material that's relevant to your message.

- Tell the joke as if it actually happened to you.

- Weave humor throughout your presentation.

- Keep your jokes short, devoid of unnecessary detail.

- Consider timing when writing and telling your joke.

HUMOR DON'TS

- Never insult your audience.

- Don't use material that doesn't fit the purpose or tone of the event.

- Keep ethnicity, religion, politics, and sexuality out of your remarks.

- Don't apologize if your joke falls flat. Move on.

- Never build up a joke before you tell it.

The many ways to get a laugh

Jokes / Anecdotes / Proverbs / Quotations

Props / Funny words / Riddles

using quotations

A well-chosen quotation can knock the socks off your audience. It can inspire, educate, surprise, delight, and make a long-lasting positive impression—of both you and your talk. Quotes that relate directly to your topic can lend credibility and importance to your subject. But quotes that expand on or complement ideas that are peripherally addressed in your talk are just as meaningful.

For example, you've been asked to give a talk to a group of product development managers. Your topic: harnessing creativity in the workplace. Imagine your audience's delight when you share quotes that illustrate what happens when product innovation is not embraced:

- "The problem with television," wrote a *New York Times* reporter in 1939, "is that the people must sit and keep their eyes glued on a screen; the average American family hasn't time for it."

- "What use could this company make of an electrical toy?" said the president of Western Union in 1876 when he turned down exclusive rights to the telephone offered by Alexander Graham Bell for $100,000.

- "A cookie store is a bad idea," wrote a potential investor in response to a business plan he'd received from Mrs. Debbi Fields. "Besides, the market research reports say America likes crispy cookies, not soft and chewy cookies like you make."

Don't feel compelled to open your talk with a quote from some ancient Greek philosopher who nobody's heard of. (Former President George H. W. Bush once told his speechwriter, "Don't ever give me any more quotations by that guy Thucydides.") Use the quote if it clarifies, illuminates, or reinforces your point, and share it with your audience the way you'd share it with a friend.

ASK THE EXPERTS

How can I comfortably quote Parmenides in my talk when I'm not sure anyone will know who I'm talking about?

Simply say, "An ancient Greek philosopher once said . . ." or, "A wise man once said . . ." Once you have decided not to use the author's name precisely, feel free to paraphrase or modernize the language to make your use of the quote sound completely natural.

How many quotations can I use in a speech without it sounding odd?

The answer to that is similar to Lincoln's answer when he was asked how long a person's legs should be. He replied, "Long enough to touch the ground." When you want to drive a point home, a relevant quotation is a memorable way to do it. When you want to rekindle the audience's attention, a quotation that will shake up the audience a little is a good way to do it, if it's relevant.

One of America's most gifted speakers and writers is John Gardner, a former Cabinet official and founder of the citizens' lobbying organization Common Cause. He once gave a speech to a group of management consultants on the subject of personal renewal in which he used 21 separate quotations. But all of them were folded into his remarks so skillfully that they seemed perfectly bonded to his own language.

Do I have to use the entire quotation?

No. You might decide to use just a word or two to make your point. In a speech about declining educational standards in America, you might say something like, "As the comedian Steve Allen once said, this 'dumbing down of America' strikes at the very foundations of our nation."

making it better

Tactics to bring your talk to life

After sitting through an unbearably boring presentation, Nobel laureate Albert Einstein once said, "I now have a new theory on eternity."

What would it have taken to command and keep Dr. Einstein's interest? The same thing that your audience members need: solid information that is presented in a meaningful way. Wait, don't panic. You can do this. All that is required is that you present fairly interesting information in such a way that your audience can personally relate to it.

Here are some tips to help you establish the critical connection with your audience that can mean the difference between yawns or raves. One rule of thumb: Use these tips sparingly or else they can overwhelm your presentation.

Energize your statistics

Statistics can be as dry as sand. Juice them up by presenting them graphically with PowerPoint slides (see chapter 9) or give them some perspective so your audience has a frame of reference to help them grasp the numbers.

Compare and contrast things

When you can compare or contrast your topic with powerful events, statistics, or ideas, you create a compelling association for your audience. Giving a talk on the need to bring in new technology? Tell how many man-hours the new technology will save. Speaking about the low rate of savings in U.S. households? Contrast it with the high rate of savings in Japan.

Make a joke

Few things relax a speaker and click with an audience like a well-told, relevant joke. If you are passionate about your topic and you find a joke that relates to it, you'll be able to deliver the punch line like a pro.

Quote someone

No matter how well you can say it, most likely someone else said it better. A well-placed quotation from an expert can give your talk credibility. But you can also quote sports figures, actors, and even children to drive your point home. Whatever you do, don't quote directly from the dictionary—very boring.

FIRST PERSON — DISASTER STORY

Too much of a good thing

My first big speech was a lesson in creative styling. I had to present the first-quarter earnings to a group of analysts, and I really wanted to make a good impression. I had all the facts at my fingertips, but I thought I would jazz them up a bit. I used jokes, anecdotes, quotes—you name it, I had it in there. The result? Overkill. My company's earnings got lost in all of it. Not surprisingly, few remembered anything about our company's results. How do I know? Because I had to repeat the information to six different analysts by phone the next week.

James L., Flint, Michigan

where to go for facts

**Great resources will
stir up great ideas**

Great, you're feeling a bit more inspired. Starting off with a fun fact or a well-turned joke is just the ticket to getting your presentation going. Except none spring to mind. What now? Relax. Let your local library and the Internet come to your aid and help you turn your speech from ordinary into exceptional.

For fun quotes and anecdotes:

IdeaBank

Need a great quote on teamwork? Fear? Happiness? How about an anecdote about John F. Kennedy? A pearl of wisdom from Yogi Berra? Or would you like to find out what else happened in recorded history on the day you are speaking? Enter your search words in IdeaBank's query box and the system searches its expansive database of anecdotes, quotations, jokes, excerpts, and dates for the perfect matches. While IdeaBank is a paid subscription service, there is a free trial available for professionals. (Online at **www.idea-bank.com**.)

Reader's Digest

Terrific source for humorous anecdotes, and you can bet they won't be too risqué for the room. (Online at **www.rd.com**.)

Newsweek

Quotable quotes on today's topics in *Newsweek*'s Perspectives section. (Online at **www.msnbc.com/news/NW-front_Front.asp**, select Opinion, then Perspectives.)

National Public Radio
Rich with informative, rewarding, and funny programming, and you're sure to find an idea or anecdote to build a speech around. Listen to your local member station, or log on to **www.npr.org**.

Bartlett's Familiar Quotations
An oldie but goodie, featuring thousands of quotations displayed by author chronologically, alphabetically, or by key word. (Online at many quotation resource sites, such as **www.bartleby.com**.)

For facts and statistics:

American Demographics Magazine
Filled with statistics from recent surveys on topics such as consumer behavior, business and marketing trends, and social issues. Eminently quotable.
(Online at **www.demographics.com**.)

Harper's Magazine
You'll find interesting perspectives on current and historical events at *Harper's Magazine*. The magazine's monthly "Index" is a treasure trove of interesting statistics that provide great material for any speechgiver. (Online at **www.harpers.org**.)

Encyclopaedia Britannica
This is the standard-bearer of factual information. Well written and very authoritative. (**www.britannica.com**)

Two Internet Sources
These two virtual encyclopedias can help you search out fascinating facts that relate to your presentation: **www. infoplease.com** and **www.encarta.com**.

USE FUN FACTS TO EMPOWER YOUR WORDS

Want a good example of teamwork, besides the tired old sports analogies?

■ Canada geese can fly 70% farther when they fly in formation rather than individually. Each bird's flapping wings create an updraft for the bird that follows.

■ Companies are like orchestras. The CEO is the conductor, management and staff are the musicians, shareholders are the ticket buyers, and the Board is the team of critics.

■ When spiderwebs unite, they can tie up a lion. (Ethiopian proverb)

■ A candle loses nothing of its light by lighting another candle.

■ Teams should work like a jazz band, where everybody knows the song but decisions of how to execute it are made interactively and from moment to moment.

now what do I do?

Answers to common questions

I'm afraid my audience will think that I don't take the occasion seriously if I tell a joke or humorous story. What should I do?

You're right to be concerned about how apropos a joke is to the occasion. Use your best judgment. Clearly, if the tone of the meeting is somber (difficult business results, layoffs, etc.) then humor probably shouldn't have a place in your talk.

If I use a mission statement to help me think through my presentation, won't it really limit the amount and type of content I can use?

You want your presentation to be tightly focused on your overriding objective. A mission statement can help keep you focused. How you achieve your objective is an open book—you can use humor, metaphor, anecdotes, etc. So keep your eye on the prize—your objective—but be creative in how you attain it.

How can I demonstrate to my audience that I am grateful for the invitation to address them?

One of the most effective things you can do as a speaker is to show the audience that you did your homework about them. Find out as much as you can about the host organization. Have they won any major awards recently? Championed any initiatives? If the city in which you are speaking is the host organization's home base, consider doing some research on the city's history. Local librarians and newspaper archives can be superbly helpful in this area. And don't overlook the host organization itself. Professional associations tend to have excellent resources for you to review.

I've found some interesting facts, but I am afraid they will seem boring. How can I best convey them?

Be expressive in your use of facts. Use figures of speech to add color. Here are the top three: **analogy** (comparison based on resemblance between two things); **metaphor** (using one thing to directly describe another); or **simile** (comparing two unlike things using the word "like" or "as"). For example: an analogy ("a computer and your brain operate in a similar way"); a metaphor ("the information superhighway"), and a simile ("our task force performed like a team of Olympians").

I am a consultant and have been asked by a client to give a talk on the occasion of their company's 50th anniversary. What should I do?

Be inclusive. Demonstrate your knowledge of the host organization. Find out the origins of the group or industry you are addressing. Quote from the CEO's shareholders' letter in the company's most recent annual report. (Better still, cite something from the company's employee newsletter.) If it's a centuries-old industry, what else was going on in history when the industry was founded?

 **OW WHERE DO I GO?!**

CONTACTS

www.dogpile.com
A metasearch engine that scans 16 separate search engines with one query, including AltaVista, Direct Hit, and others.

www.rhymezone.com
Instant thesaurus, rhyming diction-ary, homonym, synonym, and antonym finder.

www.notmuch.com
Very funny, totally unscientific polls with a down-home flavor.

www.salon.com
Sophisticated and intelligent online magazine filled with fresh ideas on people, politics, sex, and business.

www.pbs.org/greatspeeches
Plenty of inspiration here—great 20th-century American speeches in text and video.

CHAPTER 3

Writing your talk out

Outline your talk
Draw a road map of your speech **38**

Organize your points
How to structure your key points **40**

The basic outline
Fill in the blanks and you're off **42**

A basic speech
A sample speech with notes **44**

Writing for the ear
How to write like you talk **46**

Your opening
Make a strong impact **48**

The body of your talk
Putting the key points together **50**

Making it flow **52**

Revising your talk **53**

The wrap-up
Ending it like a pro **54**

Handling a Q&A session
It's easier than you think **56**

Now what do I do?
Answers to common questions **58**

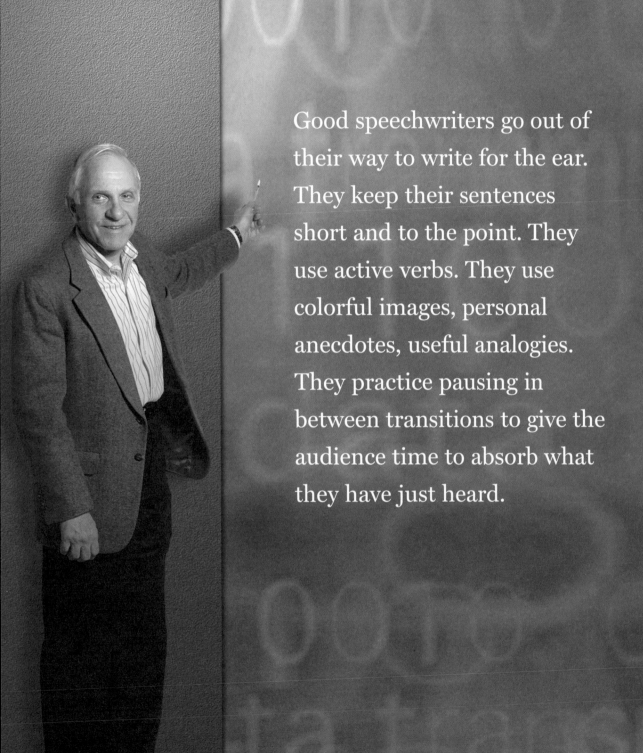

Good speechwriters go out of their way to write for the ear. They keep their sentences short and to the point. They use active verbs. They use colorful images, personal anecdotes, useful analogies. They practice pausing in between transitions to give the audience time to absorb what they have just heard.

outline your talk

First, outline your talk with a broad brushstroke

OK, you know everything you need to know about the audience you'll be addressing. Great, that's the first step. And you've figured out your **mission statement**—the one thing you want them to take away from your presentation. (For more on that see page 22.) You've done some incredible research—even learned things that fascinated you, the expert on the subject! You found a few quotes that not only captured the essence of your ideas but expanded on them in fun and surprising ways. Life is good. But wait—now it's time to take pencil to paper and write out your talk.

Don't panic. It's easier than you think. The best way to start is with a broad outline of your talk, which you will then fill in with detail. Think of this outline as a road map that will take you from Place A: your talk objective, to Place B: actually achieving it. Along the way, you'll make a few stops: The Attention-Getting Opener, Key Point 1, Key Point 2, Key Point 3, Wrap-up, a few Q&A's, and then the Knock 'Em Dead Closer. And at each of these stops, you'll see some amazing scenery: anecdotes, jokes, facts, analogies, and stories that truly make the trip memorable. Read on and see how fun the drive can be.

ASK THE EXPERTS

Should all presentations fit the same format?

You may find yourself giving a talk about a historical or current event, and you may want to present the facts in chronological order. If you are talking about an economic crisis in Russia, you may want to compare their crisis to situations in two other countries. But no matter what your topic is, keep in mind the following time-honored formula. It works like a charm:

1. Tell 'em what you're going to tell them.

2. Tell 'em.

3. Tell 'em what you told them.

I am giving a time-management presentation to a group of computer scientists. Is it a good idea to include some of their technospeak in my talk?

Only if you're sure you know the meaning of the term, use it infrequently, and in a fun or lighthearted way. It can show your audience that you thought enough of them to learn a bit about their business. However, your best bet is to avoid jargon altogether in favor of clear, simple, conversational language. If you are addressing a highly specialized or educated audience, speak to their level of sophistication but don't try to adopt their internal language.

organize your points

Choose the pattern that fits your talk

The crux of your presentation will be the two to five key points you want to make. If you've done your research, you know what those points are. Great. You're good to go. But wait a minute. How do you want to present those points? You have five organizing patterns to choose from:

Chronological Here the points flow in order of when they happened. This pattern is good for presentations where you are explaining how something happened, for example, how your division managed to increase profits by 50%.

Spatial Use this pattern when you need to give directions. For example, in a presentation on how to build a house, you would discuss how the various parts fit in space: left, right, top, bottom.

Causal If one thing is caused by another, it is considered a causal relationship. Use this pattern if your points fit into an if/then sequence. Some presentations require this organization if one key point directly leads to another, e.g., if sales don't improve, then we will have to discontinue our line.

Problem/Solution The best one to use if you are describing an existing problem and then giving the solution. This is ideal for presentations where you wish to persuade your audience to take a certain action.

Topical Let your points guide your organization in a natural progression that you choose. This open-ended pattern is good for more open-ended subjects, such as increasing membership in a company savings program.

ASK THE EXPERTS

How do I know which style is best for my presentation?

Let your key talking points be your guide. If they need to be in a certain order, then it's chronology. If it's more open-ended, and the points can be interchangeable, then you're looking at a topical organization.

Is one style of organization better than another?

Not really. The best presentation is the one that makes the most sense and is the most easily understood. If you are looking to persuade your audience, then consider the problem/solution pattern. It packs a powerful punch.

FIRST PERSON DISASTER STORY

Big Words, Small Presentation

It was my first major presentation to a large group of colleagues. I remember peppering my speech with big words that I thought would make me sound smart. It was going pretty well until I used the word "imprimatur." It's a fancy word for approval that I found in the thesaurus. I mispronounced it and heard a chuckling in the audience. After that, I felt like a fraud in front of the group, and I stumbled through the rest of my talk. It was a hard lesson to learn about just keeping things simple.

Deirdre R., Portland, Oregon

the basic outline

Here's how it looks

Here's a speechwriter's outline.

Opener Figure on devoting 10% of your speaking time to your opening remarks. Here's where you grab your audience's attention, convey a sense of trust, and prepare them for where you want to take them during your talk. Include a quote, anecdote, humor, or analogy. Think of the opener as the small talk we all engage in when we first meet someone.

Transition One sentence or two that moves you out of opening pleasantries and into your mission statement.

Mission statement/Theme Tell them what your mission is—the purpose of your talk. Make sure they understand what you want them to do, learn, or know at the end of your presentation.

Transition One sentence that lets you gracefully launch into the body of your speech.

Body You should expect to devote about 75% of your time to the body of your talk. Organize your information into no more than five key points. Important tip: Do not present your key points in a journalistic style, that is, from most important to least important— you'll lose your audience to the predictability. Instead, sandwich your less important points between the two most key points.

Wrap-up Spend about 15% of your talk time on your closing. Here you'll want to restate your mission statement and discuss how your key points support your audience's taking a particular action (or changing an opinion, or learning a new database, or purchasing a new mainframe, or . . .), then finish up with a powerful idea that captures the essence of your talk.

Questions and Answers If you choose to leave time for questions and answers, that amount of time is contingent upon the length of your presentation. If your talk took 30 minutes and covered a great deal of ground, then be sure to leave 10 minutes for questions and answers.

Knock 'em dead takeaway Don't just abruptly end your presentation with Q&A. Once you've signaled an end to the questions, end your presentation by thanking your audience for their time and then give a thought-provoking reprise of your conclusion.

a basic speech

Here's a condensed real-life sample

THE OPENER

Thank you, Jim, for your generous introduction, and good evening everyone. I am delighted to see such a strong turnout tonight in support of your foundation. And I promise to try to follow Benjamin Disraeli's advice to be amusing, never tell unkind stories, and above all, never tell long ones . . .

TRANSITION

. . . I am especially pleased to have been asked to address your group, because as a corporate CEO, I experience every day the conflict of managing corporate philanthropic programs while also trying to build record profitability . . .

MISSION STATEMENT

. . . The term "corporate philanthropy" may seem to some—particularly shareholders—to be an oxymoron. But I don't think so. While I believe most corporate giving is, and should be, in the interest of the company, I also believe it is born of enlightened, strategic thinking . . .

TRANSITION

. . . Take a look at the differences between how companies and individuals donate money . . .

BODY

. . . When was the last time you heard of a company donating money anonymously? Yet wealthy individuals often support nonprofits on the condition that they not be identified. Does that mean a corporation's gift is less meaningful than an individual's anonymous donation?

Another difference: When an individual makes a donation, no one questions their right to give their money away. No one questioned the Vanderbilts, Whitneys, Rockefellers, Astors, or Goulds. All were extremely wealthy, and all were extremely generous.

But in corporations, donation decisions are not made by the "true owners" of the money—its shareholders. Instead, employees decide where donations should be directed. Some of our shareholders are still building their wealth, and they may not be in a position to be as philanthropic as they might like to be one day. So does a corporation really have the right to give money away that technically doesn't belong to it?

BODY

And when you think of it, not only was the right of the old rich to donate their wealth not questioned, but their motivation was never an issue. They gave money to causes that were important to them, such as the arts, culture, and education. But with corporations, it's sometimes hard to see a connection between a business entity and a charitable one. There's rarely a direct benefit to the company's bottom line, so what's the motivation? Should corporate donations be viewed skeptically because there seems to be an ulterior motive?

WRAP-UP

Do the words "corporate" and "philanthropy" really cancel each other out? I don't think they do. While I believe most corporate giving programs are, and should be, in the interest of the company, I also believe it is an interest born of enlightened, strategic thinking. I have always felt that by strengthening the fabric of society—promoting financially sound communities, shoring up its educational facilities, providing funding for worthwhile causes that deserve a chance—a company can only strengthen the threads of its own human fabric.

Q&A

I'd like to take any questions now if there are any.

CLOSING

In closing, I'd just like to say that Cimter's corporate mission is to promote prosperity in communities around the world. Our philosophy toward charitable giving is inextricably linked with our corporate mission. But prosperous communities are not only those with high incomes. They are those with safe water, roads, bridges, and homes. They are communities with access to the best educational resources available. They are communities that can offer special services for the disabled, and can provide an improved quality of life for those with special needs.

That takes a lot of money. I'm proud that Cimter is in a position to support such efforts, and I truly believe that it is in our best interest to serve the public interest.

Thank you very much.

writing for the ear

There is a difference between the written and spoken word

Before you take out your trusty pad and paper and start writing out your presentation, stop and take a moment to reflect on what you are trying to accomplish. Are you trying to write a good report that covers all your points and reads well? Or are you trying to give a good presentation that your audience will remember? The difference between the two is huge. The first is called writing for the eye—where your sentences can be as long and complex as needed. The second is called writing for the ear. This calls for a different style of writing: namely, short sentences, active verbs, simple (non-technical) vocabulary, memorable anecdotes.

Why the difference? Because the eye absorbs information much faster than the ear. Most people can read many more words per minute than they can hear per minute. The reason is simple. When you read, you can read at your own pace, stop and reread if you want, even skip ahead if you wish. Not so with hearing. The listener can only listen to one word at a time, with each word spoken in order. Listeners have to pay very close attention, and that can be draining, which explains why most people tend to daydream when they listen.

To counteract the strains on the listener, good speechwriters go out of their way to write for the ear. They keep their sentences short and to the point. They use active verbs. They use colorful images, personal anecdotes, useful analogies. They practice pausing in between transitions to give the audience time to absorb what they have just heard.

WORDING THAT WORKS
HARD FOR YOU

Use words and phrases that pack a powerful, positive punch. Wimpy language, sexist terms, corporatespeak, euphemisms, clichés, and alphabet-soup acronyms put a barrier between your message and your audience. Use colorful language in the active voice. Use the first person a lot—that means using sentences that begin with I, as in "I believe that the time has come to take action." Here are some examples of sentences that have been revised to add more impact.

Okay
The facts were gathered by the finance committee to show how our organization is doing.

Better
How well is our organization doing? New facts from the finance committee show . . .

Okay
Our market share is expected to decline if the competition introduces their beta product.

Better
We can hold on to our industry lead if we work together to fight Acme's launch of their new power sander. (Positive spin.)

Okay
I think you will agree with me.

Better
I know you will agree with me. (Strong words.)

your opening

Think of it as the beginning of a conversation

What should you say first? If dread is filling your entire being at the very thought of making an opening statement, here's an inside tip: Your opening statement is very much like what you would normally say upon meeting someone new. It's simple: When you meet someone new, you probably start out by giving your name and various particulars about yourself. Same with a presentation, but with a lot more verve. You want to get the audience's attention while you tell them who you are and why you are there. And just like in a conversation, you want to establish some kind of common ground. Ergo, your opening sentences should build rapport, find common ground, establish a connection, and hopefully, compel to action.

Here's another inside tip: Be yourself. If you feel that you are forcing your opening statement, you can be sure that your audience will feel that way too. Don't open up with an approach or style that is not natural to you. If you are very outgoing, then you may feel comfortable with a clever or funny opening. If you are the more reticent type who can never come up with a smart comeback, don't panic—use a compelling statistic or a fascinating fact to get the attention of your audience.

Your opening should not just tell why you're there and what you want to accomplish. Try to set a mood. You have an audience of humans who will warm to stories of human interest. Focus on them. Shake them up. Get them to feel, get them to laugh, get them to think. If you can do this, you'll have them in the palm of your hand.

OPENING OPTIONS

A strong opener is your ticket to a successful talk.
Here are some examples:

Rhetorical question
How many of you had pesticides for breakfast this morning?

Direct question
Did you ever find yourself a passenger in a car driven by a drunk driver?

Startling fact
Your heart stops every time you sneeze.

Humor
Thank you for that very generous introduction, Tom. I was so impressed, I thought you must be talking about somebody else.

Joke
I am delighted to be here today to talk about the added value that superb customer service can bring to any business operation. For example, just last week I received a Christmas card from the guys who collect my garbage. How smart of them, and how thoughtful, I told my wife. And I felt that way until today, when I received another card from them, but this one contained a self-addressed envelope and was stamped "2nd notice."

Anecdote
On my way here this morning, I read a line in an advertisement that directly applies to our business, and that line was, "Things of quality know no fear of time."

Historical reference
What a coincidence to be addressing a gathering of financial analysts on the feast day of St. Agabus, patron saint of fortune-tellers (February 13).

Quotation
Today I promise to take the advice of Franklin Delano Roosevelt, our 32nd President. He said, "Be sincere; be brief; be seated."

the body of your talk

Your message is more than a list of key points

While your opening statement will grab your audience's attention, the body of your talk is where the rubber meets the road. This is where you'll spend the bulk of your presentation time, delivering the three to five key points that you've winnowed out from all of your ideas, research, and experience. How important are these points? Extremely—they are the foundation upon which you build the premise of your speech. Your key points will make the difference between your succeeding or failing to accomplish the mission you've set out to achieve with your talk.

key point 1

key point 3   key point 2

How's that for pressure? Not to worry! Using a little logic and creativity, and putting your mission statement above all else, you'll do fine. You have some choices about how you want to arrange your points. They can be in chronological order (for example, a speech about marketing plans, starting with last year's, then last month's, and now this week's). Your points could be arranged by categories. For instance, in a presentation on China's technology, you could mention China's growth in consumer spending, its economy, and its technological prowess. Perhaps you would present your points in problem/solution format (e.g., the competition could gain a foothold if we don't move into their territory soon).

Whichever way you organize your key points, remember—they need to be clear, compelling, and convincing. Elaborate, explain, and illustrate them using your tools of interesting but simple language, anecdotes, jokes, quotations, etc. The body of your talk is where the action should take place—your audience will either be persuaded to your point of view or not.

ASK THE EXPERTS

Is it okay to have more than one mission statement in a presentation?

Often, speakers try to cover too much territory with their talks. They might think, "Since I have to talk anyway, I might as well present my new utilities project AND the productivity trends in my department." Don't do it. Short-term memory can hold only a few pearls of information anyway, and as the complexity of information increases, the short-term memory capacity decreases. Remember: One talk, one mission to accomplish.

How many key points can I have?

Think of the (no more than!) five key points you choose as the structure upon which you build your talk. Each point should help you build a case for your listeners to be persuaded to your point of view. If they don't move you toward that goal, they may not be critical to your talk.

Is it better to write my key points out in complete sentences, or can I just use bullets?

The answer depends completely on your level of comfort speaking in front of a crowd. If you already know that you stay calm and collected at the podium and you don't forget words, key points, or your native tongue, then bullet points are fine. However, if you don't know how you'll react, don't take a chance with bullet points. You might draw a blank; with complete sentences (make them short and in the active voice), you can always fall back on reading your text.

I've been asked to speak for 60 minutes. I only have four key points! How can I stretch my presentation to an hour?

With the proper research and creative thinking, a person can spend a very engaging and compelling 60 minutes on one key point! In your case, try breaking your presentation up. Do two points in the first session—followed by a bathroom break or interactive exercise—and cover points three and four in the second session.

making it flow

The art of transitions

Now that you have a draft of your speech outlined, an attention-getting opener, and key points, it's time to buff out the rough edges of your text. Your goal here is to make sure your ideas flow so your listeners can follow. How do you do that? With transitions—statements that tell your listeners you are going in a new direction. For example, "Now that we've explored the reason why safe water is important, I next want to cover how to make it happen."

Transitions link each of the main sections of your talk, but they do much, much more. First, they help your audience ride along with you on your train of thought. With the right transitions to connect your ideas, it will be a ride free of bumps and jolting turns. Also, transitions are like directional signs at an intersection—they help lead the audience to where the talk is headed.

Don't assume your points are so obviously related that it is redundant to link them. Don't expect your audience to make those leaps of logic—it's your job to guide them along the path of your thinking so they will reach the same conclusion (yours!) in the end.

Again, be yourself. Speak to your audience the way you would speak to a friend. That means using the active voice, where the subject of each sentence acts. If you use the passive voice, the person doing the action gets lost. Compare these two sentences and see which sounds more natural and interesting:

I will tell you the answer.

vs.

The answer will be told to you by the committee.

Also, don't choose words that are not part of your regular vocabulary. Words that are lofty, difficult, or important-sounding only serve to distance you from your audience and your audience from your goal. Simple words crafted well will be understood and remembered. That's what you need to strive for.

revising your talk

Making it sound natural

The rule of thumb is to divide your speech preparation into thirds: one third for planning, one third for writing, and one third for revising. Spending more than one third of your time on polishing your speech can mean several things: You didn't plan your speech out well, you wrote it too quickly the first time, or you used very stilted, unnatural language. Before you hunker down and spend hours polishing your speech, take a few minutes to read it out loud to yourself. As you read, mark any areas that don't sound right and focus on those first.

Revisions to make:

- Change vague examples to concrete ones.

- Change sentences written in the passive voice to the active voice.

- Define any unfamiliar terms or acronyms as soon as you say them.

- Delete any jargon or "expert" vocabulary.

- Rephrase any clichés.

- A word of caution: Obsessive rewriting can be a way to avoid fears you may have about public speaking. Fear is a normal part of public speaking; the trick is to harness that anxiety to make you a better speaker, not a better writer!

the wrap-up

End on a high note

Your closing remarks should tie your talk together into a call for action—the accomplishment of your mission. You should devote about 15% of your talk time to it. Always begin by "telling 'em what you told 'em"—summarize your key points—but do so VERY briefly. Then use any number of avenues to bring your audience around to the results you want: Remind them why your topic is important to them. Answer a question you posed at the beginning. Leave them with a great, thought-provoking quote, or tell a story that illustrates your theme. Consider displaying a key visual that you showed at the beginning of your talk to reinforce what they've learned.

Appeal to the emotional nature of your audience by inspiring them to an action, belief, understanding, or idea. Use language that paints a picture in their minds. With concluding remarks such as these, you'll make a powerful and lasting impression and end your talk on a high note. And if all goes according to plan, you'll stimulate a few thoughtful questions that you will then need to answer (see pages 56–57).

54

CONCLUDING TIPS

■ Don't start gathering up your notes, pens, or papers, or do anything else to divert attention from your final words. Better still, try to calm down and speak slowly because this is when you want to command maximum attention.

■ Don't just wait for the audience to ask questions. Invite them to ask them. Better still, tell them how long the question-and-answer period will be. Don't make up an answer if you don't know it. And don't field a question over to a colleague unless he or she has been warned in advance. Do feel free to say: "That's a good question. I don't know the answer. Let me get back to you on that."

■ Don't apologize at the end of your talk for anything that happened during your talk, for example, the lack of light in the room, talking too long, etc. Do thank whoever asked you to speak.

handling a Q&A session

Survival strategies for your Q&A

Wait, it's not over yet! How so? you ask imploringly. Well, most business presentations usually end with a question-and-answer session. If you feel a little queasy at the thought of handling a Q&A session, relax. There are a few strategies you can use to make the experience painless, and even turn it into an opportunity to shine.

First, confirm with your host (as much in advance as possible) if you even have enough time to build a Q&A session into your speech. For example, if you have a total time limit of 45 minutes, you may want to schedule 30 minutes for your talk and leave 15 minutes for Q&A. If no one asks any questions, you're done early and there's no harm done.

Second, be sure to tell your audience at the outset that there will be a question-and-answer session at the end of your talk.

Third, be sure that the room is set up for questions. Logistics are important here. If it's a very large room, will there be a microphone set up for people to walk up to and speak into? Or will there be spotters in the audience to bring microphones to the questioners? If you don't have the luxury of either, be sure to repeat the question after it is asked, even gently rephrase it to your liking. This way, you'll not only clarify the question asked and ensure that your audience heard it, but you'll buy some valuable time to formulate the answer.

Fourth, save a few minutes for a final knock 'em dead closer after your Q&A is complete. The last words your audience should hear is your profound final thought—a memorable quote, philosophy, or idea that will stay with your audience for days, months, or years. If that proves to be just too much for you, a simple thank-you will do.

DOS AND DON'TS OF Q&A'S

- Repeat the question, unless you're in a small meeting room.

- If you know the person's name, use it.

- Be courteous—let the person finish his or her question.

- Maintain eye contact with the questioner while the question is being asked.

- Resume eye contact with the audience while you answer it.

- If you don't get any questions but want to expand on a particular point, say, "In the past I've been asked about . . ."

- If you don't know the answer, tell the questioner that you will find out and get back to him or her and follow up.

- When it's time to end the Q&A, let your audience know that you have time for one last question.

- After the Q&A session, wrap up your talk with a knock 'em dead conclusion.

- Interrupt the questioners, unless they are speechifying.

- Ask if you've answered a question. Move on to the next question.

- Apologize if you don't know the answer.

- If you don't know the answer, don't call on a colleague to answer it unless you've warned them in advance.

now what do I do?

Answers to common questions

Why can't I talk off the top of my head?

You've been given a precious thing: time to share your knowledge on a topic with a group of (hopefully) motivated listeners. Use this time wisely. Without notes or a script to guide you, you may float off topic and forget key points, leaving the impression among your listeners that you are not as professional or as expert as advertised. By outlining a powerful opening, the key points you want to cover, and a strong conclusion, you greatly increase the likelihood that your talk will be cohesive, comprehensive, and understood.

I have no idea what to do for the "big opening" statement. How can I come up with something that doesn't sound forced or phony?

First, be yourself. If you feel that you are forcing your opening statement, you can be sure that your audience will feel that way too. The best way to prepare your opening is to remind yourself of the mission of your talk. Think about the benefits that your point of view will provide. What will your audience miss out on if they don't accept or understand these benefits? Instead of telling them what they stand to gain by listening to you, tell them what they could lose by NOT listening.

Should I memorize my talk?

NO! That's an invitation to disaster. You'll sound robotic, stiff, and uncomfortable—hardly the image you want to project. Your goal is to be yourself up there—natural, conversational, engaging, and enthusiastic. A recited speech will surely put a wall up between you and your audience. And what happens if you lose your place and flub your lines? You won't get a second, third, or fourth take as actors do.

If there are a lot of questions, doesn't that mean that my audience didn't understood me?

Listen to what they are asking. Their questions will indicate whether they are confused or interested. If there are no questions, be alert to the activity in the audience. Are they focused on you, relaxed in their seats, even smiling? Or are they fidgeting, avoiding your eyes, collecting their things? The first group got your message. The second group can't wait to get out. While Simon and Garfunkel may have romanticized the "sound of silence," it can be deafening at the end of a presentation.

I have way too much material to cover in the 30 minutes I've been allotted for my speech. How can I cover it all?

The first thing you should do is imagine yourself seated in the audience, about to hear the third or fifth or tenth presentation of the day, and knowing it's going to be jammed full of data. Doesn't feel good, does it? Do your audience a favor: Keep your talk to one theme or mission, pare your material down to five key points—no more—and distribute a handout after your presentation containing more comprehensive detail than you covered in your talk. Above all, if you find yourself pressed for time, NEVER rush through your key points. Instead, plan in advance to finish early. One of the best gifts you can give an audience is an early ending.

NOW WHERE DO I GO?!

PUBLICATIONS

Speak Smart
by Thomas Mira

Schaum's Quick Guide to Great Presentation Skills
by Melody Templeton
and Suzanne Fitzgerald

CHAPTER 4

How to say it

To read or not to read
You decide what is most comfortable **62**

Notes for emphasis
Marking up your speech **64**

Your voice
How clear speaking can make a difference **66**

Your breathing
Breathing like a pro **68**

Vocal tools
Why voices sound different **70**

Fixing common speech faults
Get rid of annoying speech habits **72**

Rehearsing your speech
Practice does make perfect **74**

Now what do I do?
Answers to common questions **76**

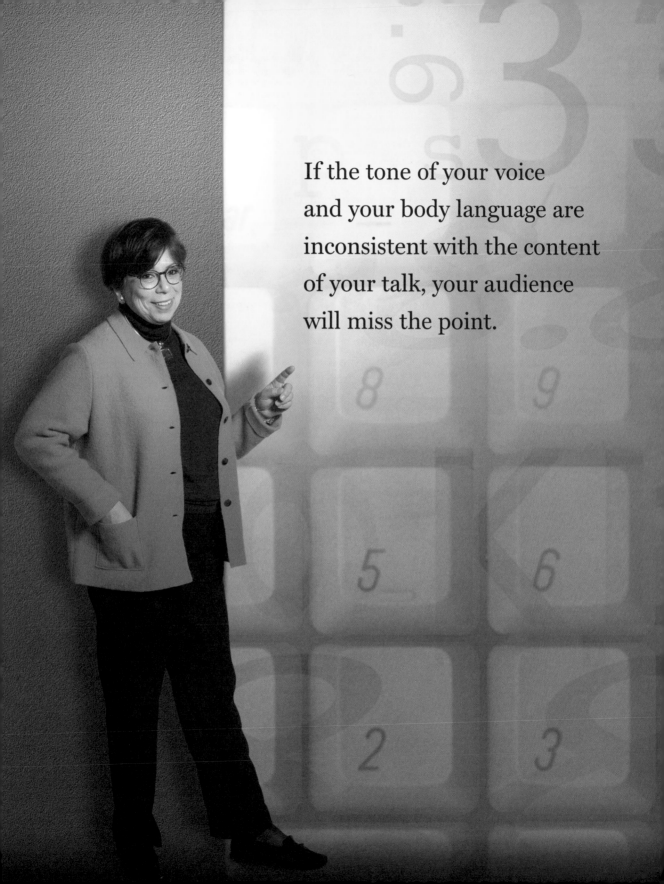

If the tone of your voice and your body language are inconsistent with the content of your talk, your audience will miss the point.

to read or not to read

You can work from brief notes or read the full text

With an outline of your talk polished and ready, you now must decide if you want to address your audience from bulleted note cards (giving a more extemporaneous talk), or if you want to read the verbatim text from a fully written speech. Both methods have pros and cons.

For example, when you work from note cards, you stand a better chance of sounding natural, interested, and confident. However, there's a danger of losing your place or not keeping track of time when you work from notes. Some presenters find that if they blank out during their talk, it is harder to resume speaking when working from a bulleted point rather than a complete sentence. But you can avoid these pitfalls by preparing note cards that clearly list your key points in order and that contain enough words to jog your memory should you start to blank out.

There are times when it makes perfect sense to read a fully written speech. If you are terrified, for example. It's a comfort just knowing that the words are always right there in front of you if you are certain that you cannot speak extemporaneously in front of an audience. Or if your talk has some legal or political content, or you may be quoted by the press where accurate wording is imperative, then you're better off reading a script. Remember, you don't have to sound like an automaton if you're reading your text. You are telling a story, and you should use your voice as a tool to generate interest and emphasis, and to engage your listeners with your enthusiasm. It is imperative if you read that you lift your eyes frequently to the audience.

To read, or not to read? A question you now can answer.

POINTERS ON NOTE CARDS

■ Use 3x5 or 4x6-inch index card–sized note cards.

■ Print large.

■ Include a transition card between each section of your talk.

■ Be neat.

■ Number the cards.

■ Write on only one side of the card.

■ When reading quotes, hold the card up so your audience sees you are reciting an exact quote.

■ Practice at least five times—long enough to know each card's main point at a glance, but not to memorize the words.

POINTERS ON SCRIPTED SPEECH

■ Use white $8\frac{1}{2}$x11-inch paper. Type on one side of the page, double spaced with wide margins.

■ Use a large typeface (16 or 18 pt. type) in upper- and lowercase. You can get lost in words typed in all uppercase.

■ Always end the page two thirds of the way down, to prevent you from looking down while reading.

■ Number each page.

■ End each page with a complete paragraph, thought, or sentence.

■ Include directions such as (PAUSE for APPLAUSE) or (PAUSE for LAUGH) but set them off with italics or parentheses.

■ Don't staple your speech. Silently slide each page from left to right as you finish reading it, or use a three-ring binder to quietly turn the pages.

notes for emphasis

Cue yourself with a marked script

If you choose to read from a typed manuscript, take a few minutes to run through the text and mark it with cues (little directions) to note where you want to slow down, speed up, emphasize certain words, pause, or relax.

Cue creatively. Use colored pens and highlighters to stress specific words. You can even write reminders to yourself in the margins (e.g., "Slow down," "Almost done," or "Relax and smile!") Tape a small photo of a friend or your child at the bottom of a page. The sight of something so familiar and comforting can ease your jitters.

Don't type your reminders or cues into your speech—handwrite them in. Your own handwriting on a typed manuscript will visually set the cues apart from your text and force you to take notice as you read.

If you speak from note cards, colored pens and highlighters can be your best friends. By underlining or circling your key points or highlighting your call to action, you'll remember where to place your emphasis.

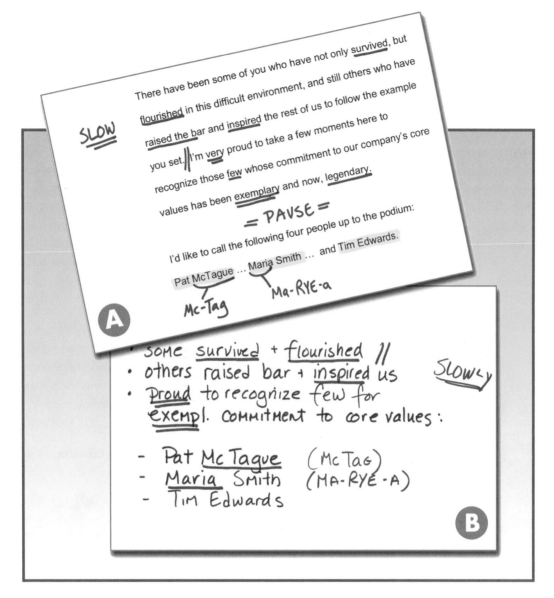

A Here's a manuscript with a variety of cues and reminders. Use any marks that work for you.

B When you work from notes, cues can help you emphasize your key points.

your voice

Understand the power of your voice

How you say it counts as much as, or more than, what you say. It may seem unfair that after all the energy and thought you put into preparing your talk, you need to be concerned about how you sound when you deliver it. But U.C.L.A. research shows that if your tone of voice and your body language are inconsistent with the content of your talk (e.g., if you speak in a monotone all hunched over the podium while announcing that your division has won a distinguished-quality award), your audience will miss the point.

Learning how your voice works can help you improve how much your audience retains of your presentation. Sounds are created as exhaled air passes through your vocal cords. Air journeys up from the lungs and into the vocal cords, which vibrate and create sound waves. These sound waves deepen and become more resonant as they reach the resonating chambers of the chest, throat, mouth, and nose, and are formed into words by the mouth and tongue.

With practice, you can train your voice to be more effective, enabling you to deliver a talk that hits the bull's-eye with your audience. Read on and learn how.

SPEECH EXERCISES

Speech coaches use a variety of speech exercises to demonstrate to their students the power of their vocal tools. Here are some of the basic ones.

To practice changing the pitch of your voice, try reading or saying a simple children's rhyme in a high-pitched voice and then trying it in a low-pitched voice. The next step is to mix the two. The goal is to train your ear to hear the difference.

To demonstrate the power of tone, try the following. Read the back of a cereal box in a flat monotone voice. If you do this correctly, you will feel a bit down and bored at the end of the reading. Now read it with as much positive emphasis as possible. How do you feel? A bit more cheerful? Notice the difference in how you feel after the two readings. Which would you prefer your audience feel?

To experience how inflection can alter the meaning of a word or phrase, read the following sentences out loud, putting emphasis on different words as you read:

<u>I</u> didn't say you hurt my feelings.   **(Someone else said it.)**

I <u>didn't</u> say you hurt my feelings.   **(Strong denial.)**

I didn't <u>say</u> you hurt my feelings.   **(I might have suspected it . . .)**

I didn't say <u>you</u> hurt my feelings.   **(Someone else hurt them.)**

I didn't say you <u>hurt</u> my feelings.   **(You just bruised them a little . . .)**

I didn't say you hurt my <u>feelings</u>.   **(You hurt my ego, though.)**

To reveal the art of articulation, try the age-old trick of speaking with a mouthful of bubble gum (three or four pieces). If you can be understood by a friend as you speak with a mouthful of gum, then your articulation without it is assured.

fixing common speech faults

Overcoming bad habits

Some years ago, a Gallup poll surveyed what annoys people most about other people's voices. Mumbling and talking too softly topped the list, followed by yelling, speaking in a monotone, using "um," "like," and "uh," a nasal voice, talking too fast, bad grammar, and a high-pitched voice.

Though you may think you fall into one of these categories, don't panic just yet. First, assess the situation. Get a tape recorder and record your voice. How you sound on tape is not exactly how you sound to an audience, but it will most likely reveal a few common speech flaws:

Mumbling The best way to knock speech fillers (such as the ever-popular "um" or "ah") out of your talk is to tape yourself and study how often, and especially where, you use these fillers. Look for patterns. If you find you use them

before you pronounce an unfamiliar word or prior to introducing each key point, you may want to adjust your vocabulary or transitions to help you glide through your talk filler-free. Another technique is to pause when you feel a filler coming on. Pausing will help you replace the speech filler with a breath. It also offers the benefit of commanding your audience's attention.

Upward inflection This is normal when you ask a question. But if you do this with statements, record yourself with the aim of listening and practicing till you get rid of that invisible question mark. Another tip: Cue your script with a symbol in the margin (a downward arrow, for example) to remind yourself not to inflect skyward at the end of each sentence.

Nasal voice A voice sounds "nasally" when the sound waves traveling up from your chest have more resonance in the nose and not enough in the mouth. It could be caused by a tightening of the lower jaw, which tenses the throat muscles. Or you may be bunching your tongue at the back of your mouth so it blocks the passage of sound into your mouth and forces it into your nose.

High pitch A high-pitched voice. To fix it, remember to do your deep-breathing exercises (stomach out, chest in). The deeper you breathe (which helps your diaphragm massage your lungs), the more relaxed you'll feel, and your voice will become richer and fuller.

Poor articulation Not pronouncing words clearly and succinctly makes an audience work much harder than they need to or want to. Plus, you leave the impression that you don't really care if you are being understood. By slowing down and really thinking about each word and point you are making, you stand a much better chance of communicating clearly.

Inappropriate gestures Nervous tics such as finger drumming, lip biting, and coin jingling can drive an audience mad. To limit such fidgety behaviors, you need to be aware of them. Record yourself on videotape to isolate your fidgets, and practice your talk as you consciously try to rid yourself of these tics. A cue in the margin (i.e., "DON'T FIDGET") can't hurt, either.

rehearsing your speech

Practice, then rehearse, to make perfect

If you are wondering whether you need to practice and rehearse your presentation, stop. You do. Period. The phrase "wing it" should not even enter your mind, unless preceded by the word "don't."

How does practice differ from rehearsal? When you practice your talk, your focus is on content and emphasis. You fine-tune any phrasings, transitions, jokes, and ideas that don't quite work. You time your talk to make sure it's within the parameters you've been given. You figure out which words you'll emphasize and where you'll build in pauses. You practice your jokes. You study yourself on tape to ensure that you speak clearly, without fillers such as "ah," "uh," and "like."

Rehearsal takes all of these things into consideration, but also includes the physical aspects of your talk if you are using visual aids. For example, rehearsing your talk lets you know when to advance your slides as you speak, or use a laser pointer or remote mouse. (For more on visual aids, see pages 126–146.) If you have access to the room in which you'll be speaking, get familiar with the stage, podium, and microphone. You should do at least one full rehearsal with all your technical devices, though it doesn't matter if you can't rehearse from the stage on which you'll be speaking. As long as you are comfortable with your talk and your technology tools, you'll communicate your confidence when you speak.

ASK THE EXPERTS

How many times should I rehearse my speech?

Experts suggest no more than four or five times. More than that and you will lose your enthusiasm for your talk.

How important is it to rehearse in the room in which I'll be speaking?

Sometimes it's not an option—the room simply may not be available to you for a rehearsal. What's more important, though, is that you get to the room early to become familiar with it. Spend some time chatting with the technicians who will be operating your slides or the person who will be recording the speech. Shake hands with members of the audience when they arrive. You'll feel much more comfortable once you've seen the room layout and met the people who make up your audience.

FIRST PERSON   DISASTER STORY

Rehearsal overload

When I got to the banquet hall, I had a chance to rehearse my speech for the tenth time that day. The projector was in place, and my slides were all in order, but my speech was awful. I decided to rewrite it at the last minute. What a mistake. The slides didn't go with my new speech, and I kept stumbling over my words. A colleague who had been kind enough to hear my practice read of my speech that morning asked what happened. I told him that I had rewritten it at the last minute. He said he thought the first speech was really good. I guess I had rehearsed so much that I found my words boring. I forgot the audience hadn't heard them ten times.

Mike K., Chappaqua, New York

now what do I do?

Answers to common questions

I have a distinct southern accent. What can I do about it?

Speech therapists and coaches can help you, and often English as a Second Language (ESL) departments at colleges in your area will offer courses in accent reduction. However, these programs can run several months and several hundreds of dollars. If you're not interested in spending that much time or money, you could purchase accent-minimizing audiocassettes from a company such as Dialect Accent Specialists Inc., in Lyndonville, Vermont (**www.dialectaccentspecialists.com**).

I tend to mumble a lot. I have tried everything, but can't seem to break this habit.

Ask yourself if it's just a bad habit or perhaps a symptom of something deeper. People with low self-esteem often mumble because they are convinced no one is interested in what they have to say. But their mumbling makes listening very difficult, so people turn away. It's a vicious cycle. To break it, try talking about something you really care about and are personally committed to.

Should I define acronyms when I use them?

Good speakers never assume the level of knowledge of their audience. It's always a good idea to define acronyms or technical terms in your talk. You need only define them once, when you first use them.

A friend said I should try to pretend I am having a conversation when I give my talk. Is that good advice?

Yes. "Dialoguing" with your audience will make each attendee feel that you are speaking directly with him or her. You can accomplish this with good eye contact, conversational speech, and a comfortable stance. Try being interactive with your group—ask for a show of hands, single a few people out by first name, and most important, speak from your heart. People connect with sincerity, and they will come away from your presentation feeling as if they'd had a conversation with you.

How can I sound polished if I'm asked to give impromptu remarks? There's no time for rehearsal!

It's hard enough to speak to a group when you've planned your comments and rehearsed them. Addressing an audience without any advance notice can be even more intimidating. Hopefully, you'll have a minute or two to gather your thoughts. Jot down what your most important idea is, and open with it. Add two more points to complement it. Your transitions can be as simple as, "My second point is . . ." Finally, close with a call to action, a question, or a word of thanks for being asked to speak. Impromptu speaking is not the easiest thing to do. Even Mark Twain had a problem with it. He said, "It usually takes more than three weeks to prepare a good impromptu speech."

NOW WHERE DO I GO?!

CONTACTS	PUBLICATIONS
www.breathing.com	**Speaking Up** by Janet Stone and Jane Bachner
www.deepsloweasy.com	**How to Write and Deliver an Effective Speech** by Judith A. MacManus
www.voicecoach.net	
www.creatingvoices.com	**The Presentation Skills Workshop: Helping People Create and Deliver Great Presentations** by Sherron Bienvenu
	The Articulate Executive by Granville N. Toogood

CHAPTER 5

Appearances matter

Your entrance
How to make it memorable **80**

Body language
You want it to match your words **82**

Eye contact
It's not as scary as you think **84**

Your personal style
Putting your best foot forward **86**

Your dress
Be sure to fit the occasion **88**

Now what do I do?
Answers to common questions **90**

BODY DOS

■ Use natural movements you'd use in conversation, but make them a bit more broad, consistent with the size of your audience.

■ Keep elbows bent with your hands resting on the podium or gesturing. It's a more open, energetic position than just letting your arms hang.

■ Vary your hand gestures. Put your hands in your pockets or hold a pencil—but limit the time you do so.

■ Stand a bit back from the podium so your head isn't bent over to read your text.

■ Move! Not while making your key points, but during the segues between them.

■ Stand tall and confidently.

BODY DON'TS

■ Don't force your smile.

■ Don't rock back and forth or shift your weight from leg to leg at the podium.

■ Don't let your arms droop at your sides.

■ Don't slump your shoulders or cross your arms over your chest.

■ Don't jiggle coins in your pockets.

■ Don't assume the "soccer penalty kick" posture, with hands clasped in front of you defensively.

■ Don't point your finger at anyone in the audience, ever—even in a friendly way.

eye contact

Lock them in with your eyes

If the eyes are indeed the windows to the soul, you can bet that your audience will have a pretty good idea of what's going on in your head (i.e., nervous, sincere, scared, ready) just by how much or how little you engage them with your eyes. Good eye contact can help you establish a connection with your audience—a bond—that even the most profound speech alone can't do. It's a way to create the feel of a one-to-one conversation.

But meaningful eye contact is not scanning your audience, where you quickly glance across a row or section of the room. Nor is it

staring, which you may find yourself doing without realizing it. Meaningful eye contact means holding the gaze of one member of your audience for up to 10 seconds—just enough time to finish a thought, register an idea, maybe even receive feedback (a nod, a smile) from the listener. Then move on to another person. Seek out people from all sections of the room. If it's appropriate, smile while you connect visually with them. If a person you're trying to connect with looks away, don't take it personally. It's a pretty good bet he's uncomfortable with your attention. Just turn to another person.

Remember, you can reveal even more than your soul through your eyes. They can also communicate your enthusiasm, professionalism, and competence.

ASK THE EXPERTS

How can I keep meaningful eye contact if I'm trying to read my speech?

There's an art to this, and it involves practice, practice, practice, till you are utterly familiar with your script. When you begin your presentation, you want to establish eye contact right away. It could be while you thank the person who introduced you, or you might just dive right into your blockbuster opening statement—but you should be speaking to a person, not to your typed speech. This means you need to be so familiar with your opening that you could recite it if you had to—at least the first sentence or two.

During the body of your speech, you should, with one glance at your text, be able to recite from memory the beginning of each paragraph or section in your speech. Make eye contact with your listeners as you say your lines, then glance down to continue the speech. Look up, then down. The key thing is to engage your listeners with your eyes while you are sharing a thought or an idea. Lock onto them to make your point, and you'll make a powerful connection.

FIRST PERSON DISASTER STORY

If the shoe doesn't fit, don't wear it

I didn't appreciate how important body language was to the art of speaking until I had to fly out to speak at a fancy business dinner on short notice. The men were all dressed in business black tie—dark suits and ties; the women were in evening wear. I realized too late that I had forgotten to pack my dress shoes and only had my beat-up loafers. The concierge managed to find me a pair of dress shoes, but they were two sizes too small. They were so painful to stand in that I was unconsciously cringing throughout my entire talk. Afterward, a few friends came up and asked what was wrong. I didn't realize how much those shoes had interfered with my ability to communicate. I should have just worn my loafers and been comfortable.

Sam K., Memphis, Tennessee

your personal style

Let the best "you" shine through

Right now you're probably thinking, "I have to let my personality come through my talk? I'm going to have enough trouble just getting through the presentation!" But whether you like it or not, your personal style of delivery will have as much of an impact—or more—than your words alone. In fact, some studies on communications effectiveness show that what is actually said in a presentation (your words) counts for as little as 10% of overall impact, while how you say it (your delivery) commands 90%. Yikes!

Fortunately, there are ways to improve your physical presence. For starters, when you walk up to that podium, try to present the very best that you are. Your enthusiasm, respect, professionalism, warmth, insight, and humor will contribute toward the charisma that can gain you so much. You've heard it before: Be yourself up there. Let the special person that you are shine through.

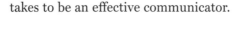

First impressions are powerful audience influencers. Through your sound and movement onstage, your audience gets a powerful sense of who you are and what your potential is. They pick up on your unique vision, your ability to relate to people, and your professionalism in a tense situation. In short, they can see if you have what it takes to be an effective communicator.

ASK THE EXPERTS

How can I prevent my nervousness from being the only thing people remember about my presentation?

You need to have confidence in your presentation first, and the confidence to deliver it will follow. Polish your presentation until you have a terrific script, full of interesting language and ideas. Practice it till you are comfortable with every part of it. Know the middle and end of it as well as you know the beginning. Be "in the moment" as you deliver it. Practice belly breathing (see page 68). Don't think about what you just said or what you will be saying in five minutes—think instead about what you are saying right now, and put your passion behind it as you say it. That's how your personality and conviction will shine through, and that's what your audience will never forget.

How can I achieve the credibility of a person like Dan Rather?

Dan Rather didn't become what he is today after his very first broadcast, so don't put unachievable expectations on yourself. But if you analyze what makes Dan Rather such a great news anchor, you'll see that he speaks plainly and directly; he's focused, personable, and uses unique expressions that make his broadcasts memorable. His style communicates an accessible personality. Remember to let your own personality radiate through your body and your words to realize the success you want to achieve.

your dress

Your clothes should suit the occasion

Years ago, if you stood outside an IBM sales office at quitting time, you'd see a flood of blue suits, white shirts, black shoes, and rep ties come through the doors. IBM's founder, T. J. Watson, Sr., never told his employees specifically what to wear, but he made it clear that his salespeople must dress conservatively so that potential clients would not be distracted or offended by an IBMer's clothing. The blue suit ensemble became the IBM uniform.

Though dress codes have relaxed at IBM and at companies around the globe, there's a lot of wisdom behind Mr. Watson senior's edict. When you are center stage to give your presentation, whether in a conference room of 20 people or an auditorium of 200, you want people to be focused on your message, not on your outfit.

But that doesn't mean you should wear a dark blue suit or navy dress whenever you speak. In fact, if you wore an outfit like that to an off-site executive gathering where everyone else was in shorts and polo shirts, you'd look pretty silly.

The rule of thumb is this: If you are a businessperson about to address a business audience, find out from the meeting planner what the style of dress is for the event, then dress one step up. For example, if the attire is "business casual," that means some men and women may wear jackets over khakis or dark pants. A male speaker should wear a casual tie with a colored shirt and sports jacket. A female presenter could wear a colorful skirt and knit sweater. You're fitting into the category of business casual, but taking it one step better.

If you are a businessperson about to address a school or community group, wear the suit or dress you would normally wear in a meeting with an important client. You want to leave the impression of total competence and crisp professionalism, and khaki pants just won't cut it.

$\textsf{A}$SK THE EXPERTS

What's the difference between "business casual," "smart casual," "corporate casual," "casual," and regular business attire?

For sanity's sake, rest assured that there are really only three categories of corporate attire, which break out like this:

Very casual Shorts, jeans, sandals, sneakers, polo shirts, etc. Clothing you might wear to a movie or the grocery store. Typically, this dress code is reserved for off-site business meetings and Silicon Valley businesses. If you are addressing a very casually dressed group, go one better: Men and women should wear pressed khakis (NEVER shorts), and a good quality polo shirt or button-down oxford. No sneakers.

Business casual (a.k.a. "corporate casual," "smart casual," etc.) Few trends have caused more confusion in the corporate world than the shift to business casual clothing. Even today, you'll see men wearing suit pants with polo shirts as if to ensure that their outfit is at least half right. If you are addressing a business casual group, again, go one better: Men should wear slacks, a casual tie, and a colored or denim shirt with a sports jacket; women should wear a skirt or slacks, knit top or blouse, scarf, and jacket.

Business dress Today, there's a wide range of clothing that's considered formal business attire. Though still limited to suits, ties, and shirts, men finally have a wide range of colors to choose from. Women have skirt and pantsuits, and dresses. If you are addressing a group of people wearing formal business attire, dress like an IBMer in the 1950s or a banker from J.P. Morgan. Your clothing should read crisp, rich, professional, competent, and conservative—and that means dark fabrics, shined shoes, and accessories that don't distract.

now what do I do?

Answers to common questions

I submitted my own introduction in writing before my talk, but the host skipped over the most important parts. What can I do in the future if this happens again?

You did the right thing by preparing and submitting your own introduction in advance. But if it wasn't used, or the host ignored or misrepresented any part of it, don't be shy about starting off your talk with key elements of your background. Don't criticize the host (never criticize the host!); instead, say something like, "As Jim said, I was an Oxford fellow from 1985 to 1987. But after I left England, I organized clinical trials for Yale that led me to the findings I'd like to talk to you about today. . . ." You need to establish your credibility and expertise immediately up front so that the audience trusts that you are the right person to be addressing them that day.

I wear glasses. Will that impede my eye contact with my audience?

Not if you take a few simple, commonsense steps before you speak. For example, make sure your glasses fit. Are they crooked on your face? Use another pair or you'll have people staring at you for the wrong reason. If they are too loose, tighten them up so they don't slide down your nose as you glance at your script. Light-sensitive glasses will darken under a spotlight, so they're not a good choice for speech day. Try nonglare eyeglasses instead, which will minimize reflected light. And here's a tip for those nervous nearsighted folks: If you don't need your glasses to read from your notes, leave them home. Your audience will be a blur, and you are less likely to be intimidated by a room full of people you can't see!

Are there any special appearance considerations for women?

Yes, just a few.

- If you wear makeup, go easy on it—particularly eye makeup. (You'll have enough shadowing from the overhead lights!)

- Forgo shiny, dangling jewelry.

- Stiletto heels can get caught in carpet.

- If you need to clip on a microphone, wear a jacket or button-down blouse.

Are there any special dress tips for men?

■ Ties show you care about how you look, even at a very casual meeting.

■ If you are wearing formal business attire and are presenting to a group of people in casual dress, then take off your jacket and roll up your shirtsleeves to indicate that you're getting down to business and working right alongside them.

■ Shoes should always be shined.

I'm too nervous to look into people's eyes while I speak. What can I do instead?

You'll communicate your nerves if you scan the audience too quickly or avoid your listeners' eyes. A better bet would be to speak sincerely to any empty seats in the room, or to different patterns in the carpet, or to a stanchion in the aisle, or to an exit sign (though you may appear to be talking over people's heads, literally). The beauty of meaningful eye contact, even if it's with an empty chair, is that your listeners will interpret your eye contact as an attempt to communicate your sincerity, enthusiasm, warmth, and professionalism. They'll never know you weren't speaking to a human.

NOW WHERE DO I GO?!

CONTACTS	PUBLICATIONS
www.presentations.com	**Effective Presentation Skills**
www.executive-speaker.com	by Steve Mandell

CHAPTER 6

Types of talks

Types of talks
Different speeches for different needs **94**

Informational talks
Instruct and enlighten at the same time **96**

Persuasive talks
You can change people's minds **98**

Motivational talks
Making an emotional appeal **100**

Introductions
Dos and Don'ts of introducing a speaker **102**

Panelist talks
Speaking with others **104**

Being a moderator
How to facilitate at a panel **106**

Leading a seminar
Showing your stuff **108**

Now what do I do?
Answers to common questions **110**

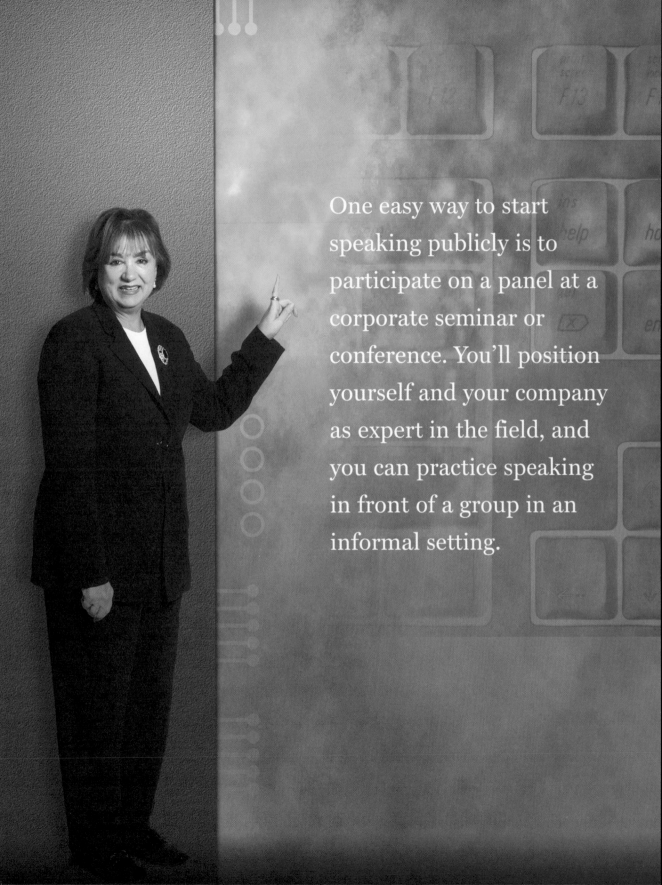

One easy way to start speaking publicly is to participate on a panel at a corporate seminar or conference. You'll position yourself and your company as expert in the field, and you can practice speaking in front of a group in an informal setting.

types of talks

Different audiences call for different speeches

During the course of your career, you may be called on to present a project update, recommend a course of action to senior management, or deliver a "state of the business" talk to shareholders. You may find yourself trying to motivate employees around a common goal, persuade potential clients to buy your product or moderate a panel of experts at an industry conference. Each of these situations calls for a different approach to the format of your speech.

Even if you have to present the same topic to different audiences, the mission of your speech and its format will vary. Here's an example: Andrea Christensen, hypothetical CEO of New York Shoes, Inc., must deliver news of a disastrous quarter to her company's constituents. When presenting the information to her board of directors, her speech will be **informational**—she'll present a detailed history of how the company got into its situation and its plan for recovery. When addressing her distribution network, her talk will be **persuasive**—she wants to assuage their concerns and reinforce the advantages of doing business with New York Shoes. Her employees are another story: She must give a **motivational** talk to inspire them to confidence in the strong foundation of the business.

Most talks fall into one of these three categories, and they are detailed for you on the following pages.

 **SK THE EXPERT**

How do I decide whether my speech should be informational, persuasive, or motivational?

Before you begin drafting any remarks, you need to decide what the mission is for your presentation. Are you there to present the history of U.S. population? That would be an informational speech. Are you trying to convince an audience that a new waste facility would lower the standard of living in your community? You'd be presenting your argument in a persuasive speech. If you want to rally a group of high school juniors to study hard for their SATs, you'd be giving a motivational talk.

Don't all speeches have a persuasive component to them?

In a way, yes. Even if you are not selling a product or asking your audience to take a specific action at the close of your speech, every talk requires that you "sell yourself." You need to persuade your audience to believe you—to believe that you are credible, competent, and expert in your topic. That doesn't mean that you should open your talk with 20 minutes on your brilliant career or vastly impressive experience—quite the contrary. Your credibility displays itself when you are fully prepared for your talk, enthusiastic, engaging, and even humble in your delivery.

informational talks

Just the facts, ma'am

Put your TV hat on for a second, and try to remember the name of the weary but dedicated detective who would say, "The facts, ma'am. Just give me the facts." Okay, enough suspense—it was Sgt. Joe Friday of *Dragnet* fame. By insisting on "just the facts," Sgt. Friday was asking his witnesses to extract all the irrelevant detail, judgment, and emotion from their accounts and provide just the information he needed to make a decision. In essence, this is what you will do when you give an informational talk.

Informational presentations enlighten, instruct, or update your audience. They should be brief and nonjudgmental; this is not the time to lay out an argument or try to persuade your audience to one side or another.

Generally, informational talk topics include descriptions of objects, processes, events, or concepts. The talk should be focused so that you can keep within the time frame you've been given to speak. If you've been given 20 minutes to talk about "population," you'll need to narrow the topic to a manageable bite, such as U.S. postwar population patterns.

The next time you find yourself wondering whether the information you're including in your informational talk should really be there, just remember Sgt. Friday's advice: "Just give me the facts."

EXAMPLES OF INFORMATIONAL TALK TOPICS

Objects
"Alternative Energy Cars" (products)
"Ellis Island" (places)

Processes
"Status Update on E-commerce Effort" (project briefing)
"Conducting Employee Reviews" (training)

Events
"The 1987 Stock Crash"
"The Semiconductor Wars"

Concepts
"Pricing Strategy and Customer Perception"
"Corporate Philanthropy"

HOW TO STRUCTURE AN INFORMATIONAL TALK

Chronological
Topic is presented in a sequence of events (i.e., describe the accomplishments leading to an employee award).

Spatial
Facts are presented in terms of their physical relationship to each other (e.g., describe the room layout for the annual company holiday party).

Causal
Data are described in terms of cause/effect; problem/solution (e.g., describe the growth in personal communications devices and its effect on telecom companies).

Topical
Information is organized and presented by subtopics within your overall speech topic (e.g., a talk on psychology is divided into cognitive, behavioral, and Freudian subtopics).

persuasive talks

Change and action are desired outcomes of persuasive speech

When it's your turn to run your company's annual volunteer appeal, you'll quickly discover the necessity and power of persuasive speech. The same is true when you lobby corporate management to switch computer platforms or when you pitch your product to your competition's clients.

Anytime you ask your audience to accept a new idea, change an existing belief, or take a course of action, you are engaging in persuasive speech. For you to succeed in persuading your audience requires that you take four steps:

- Build trust with your sincerity and credibility.
- Set out the facts to support your position.

- Be familiar with the position of the opposing side (if there is one) and anticipate and answer your audience's concerns (if possible, before they express them).
- Prompt your audience to adopt your position.

These steps create a framework for all persuasive speeches and can help you accomplish your goal of eliciting action or change within your audience.

WHAT IF

What if the audience doesn't like what I am saying?

Before you craft your persuasive speech, you must understand the composition of your audience. If it's likely that your listeners will be hostile or resistant to your proposition, you'll need to appeal to them with an ironclad case. Outline the evidence supporting your argument. Define the problem and prove how your idea is the solution. Compare the advantages of your proposal against the disadvantages of not adopting it. But remember, proposing your solution and bullying people into accepting it are two different things. Your goal is to get your audience to truly want to do what you ask them to do. If you are too forceful or patronizing, you may alienate your audience. And as John Morley, the 19th century British politician, once said, "You have not converted a man because you have silenced him."

TYPES OF PERSUASIVE SPEECHES

Experts say that persuasive speeches contain one of three different propositions:

Proposition of fact: Your speech theme would propose a debatable fact, such as "Cell phone use causes brain cancer." Your talk must contain substantial evidence to support your proposition of fact.

Proposition of value: Here you try to prove the value or worth of something. Is it good or bad, ethical or unethical, wise or foolish? An example of a speech theme that offers a proposition of value: "Personal use of corporate credit cards is wrong."

Proposition of policy: Here you propose a policy change, outline a particular course of action. Examples include, "School vouchers improve educational options," and "Pricing increases lower the quantity of clients but improve the quality of returns."

motivational talks

Appealing to emotions when teamwork is called for

Motivating employees is a subtle but necessary art. Business environments are almost always rife with uncertainty and change—rapid growth followed by layoffs; boom times followed by bust. Not surprisingly, these cycles of change can cause employees to feel distracted, demoralized, alienated, and unproductive. How can you repair "people" problems before they become fatal to the business?

Even when business is good, things can always be better: tighter expense control, more efficient production methods, better communication among teams. How can you get your employees to change what already seems to be working?

The best way is to bring people together and talk them into striving toward a common goal. Motivational speech is persuasive, but more than other types of talks, it tends to zero in on the emotions and needs of your audience. Before you address a group, you'll need to understand what makes them tick, what would drive them to accept your idea, unite with the others in the group, and move forward productively and without resentment or fear.

ⒶSK THE EXPERTS

I was never very good at psychology. How will knowing about Maslow's hierarchy help me motivate my division?

Maslow's theory stated that people's most basic needs must be met before they can address higher goals (see box at right). So, start by appealing to the lower, more physical needs first. Make sure your audience is physically comfortable. The room should not be too cold or too hot. Ideally, you should have coffee and snacks at the meeting. Then you can move onto the higher, more self-actualizing needs. Talk to them about empowerment and continuous improvement, and show appreciation for their contributions. By appealing to your group's higher needs, you may have a better shot at capturing their attention and motivating them into action.

To cut costs, I have had to lay off some members of my team. The people remaining seem to be distracted and less productive. How can I motivate them to keep production up?

This is a hard one. Layoffs often have a rebound effect. Sure, they lower costs, but they can have an unsettling effect on those who remain. There's a good chance they will be less productive because of uncertainty about their own future, concern for their peers who were let go, or resentful that their workload may increase. The key to solving this problem is communication, and lots of it. As the manager of this team, the best way to motivate your people is to bring them together to discuss their concerns openly. Be honest. Never make promises you can't keep about their job security, but appeal to their higher needs by fostering a sense of belonging (i.e., "We're in this together . . .") and stress how now, more than ever, their contributions to the firm are valued.

THE NEEDS OF YOUR AUDIENCE

It's important to remember that employees are more than "staff," "human resources," or "human capital." They are people, and all people have basic needs that must be met as they develop into fulfilled individuals.

Abraham Maslow, a 20th-century psychologist, identified a hierarchy of human needs:

■ **Physiology** (food, drink, exercise)

■ **Safety** (security, order, protection)

■ **Belonging** (sociability, acceptance, love)

■ **Esteem** (status, prestige, acknowledgment)

■ **Self-actualization** (personal fulfillment, growth)

As each need is met, beginning with the lowest, most basic physical need, the person is motivated forward to the highest need in the hierarchy, self-actualization. Think about the order of these needs as you plan your speech.

introductions

A gentle way to start public speaking

Introducing a speaker at a business event can have rewards beyond simply practicing your public speaking skills. It can create, in the minds of your audience, a perceived association between you and the speaker. Even more beneficial, it opens the door for you to cultivate a relationship with the speaker, should you choose to.

There is a certain protocol to introducing a speaker. For starters, your remarks should be brief—no more than three minutes. Pare down the speaker's official bio so that you have only the most relevant credentials to work with. Mention the name of the person right up front. Practice saying the name before you go up. After you have stated the speaker's name, give his or her title, for example, "We are very fortunate to have with us today Ms. Donna Ballinger, a senior managing director at . . ." Then cite a few of the speaker's accomplishments to show why this person is qualified to speak. Next, briefly say what your speaker's topic is, without giving it all away. Be sincere, use humor if appropriate, and don't embarrass the person with gratuitous flattery.

Finally, signal the close of your introduction with an invitation to the speaker to step up to the podium. Applaud at the podium until he or she reaches the stage, then welcome your guest with a handshake and take your seat. If the agenda permits, go back onstage when the speaker concludes to thank the person and comment on the value (always positive!) of his or her remarks.

ASK THE EXPERTS

I had the honor of introducing a real industry giant with whom I'd like to stay in touch. How do I do that without being annoying?

A very easy and nonintrusive way to stay in touch is to send a letter—not an e-mail. If the person is an industry legend, for example, and you want to encourage an association, send a personal note saying how much you enjoyed her speech and express your hopes to meet again.

I have to introduce the keynote speaker at a company meeting next week, and I just received an eight-page biography from her! How do I choose which credentials to include in my introduction?

This question calls to mind the cardinal rule in preparing any speech: Your audience comes first. Select those credentials that are most relevant or interesting to your audience. If your company manufactures chemicals and your speaker once worked for an environmental advocacy organization such as Greenpeace, that bit of information would be of interest to your audience. Remember, your speaker is more than her prepared biography. Do some research. See if you can find an anecdote about or a quote from your speaker that could be included in your introduction.

A SAMPLE SPEAKER'S INTRODUCTION

"Ladies and gentlemen, Benjamin Franklin once said that 'Glass, china, and reputation are easily cracked, and never well mended.' Our speaker today has spent the past 30 years perfecting the glue that helps repair corporate reputations in challenging times. Noah Ramsey is executive vice president of crisis communications at Turner and Sinopoli, the world's largest public relations firm. In his 20 years there, he has worked on some of the most high-profile corporate catastrophes, from the 1984 Acme oil spill in Peru to the DynaTech aspirin tainting two years ago. Before joining Turner and Sinopoli, Mr. Ramsey handled crisis strategy for Cingentian, a biotech company in Switzerland. He's here today to tell us how to prepare a disaster plan, in the hopes that we'll never need to use it. Please welcome Mr. Noah Ramsey."

panelist talks

Take every opportunity to speak to a group

The one surefire way to overcome the awkwardness (okay, terror) you may feel about public speaking is by practice. And in business, there are more than enough opportunities to practice building your skills. Don't wait till you have to present the corporate advertising strategy to the board of directors—start getting comfortable in front of groups in small, less threatening settings.

One easy way to start speaking publicly is to participate on a panel at a corporate seminar or conference. Serving as a panelist at industry events such as these is a win-win situation. You'll position yourself and your company as expert in the field, and you can practice speaking in front of a group with brief remarks in an informal and comfortable setting.

How To Do It Well

Find out the purpose of the overall event, who is in the audience, the theme of the panel, who else is serving on the panel, and what each person will discuss. You should tailor your talk to expand on the theme of the panel without duplicating another person's remarks. Use notes rather than reading a written script.

ASK THE EXPERTS

What is the best way to prepare to be a panelist?

Just as with any other presentation, you want to know who is in your audience and why they are there. Find out what the theme is for the panel, and what the other panelists will address so you don't duplicate their remarks. What makes serving on a panel different, though, is that you should view your remarks as being part of a bigger picture. Rather than dusting off a boilerplate corporate PowerPoint presentation, focus your remarks so that they specifically address what your company is doing to address the larger issues causing the problem that the panel is there to discuss.

How can I have the most impact as a panelist?

The best panelists are provocative, thorough, funny, and even aggressive. Quick wit is always appreciated by the audience, particularly when two panelists disagree on a point. Good panelists are attentive to their co-presenters, listening and responding to their remarks as a member of the audience would. They never look bored, and frequently make a point of chatting with their co-panelists before the session begins so they have a clear sense of who will be saying what. Finally, a good panelist is gracious to his or her co-presenters and never hogs the stage.

FIRST PERSON   DISASTER STORY

An underprepared panelist

I was thrilled when a good friend and colleague asked me to be part of a panel at an industry conference that she was moderating. We chatted about the panel a few times and I felt so comfortable that I didn't really prepare. I just jotted down some notes on some paper and thought I'd wing it. I was shaken to see that the other panelists had prepared PowerPoint slides and had handouts for the audience. I wish I had asked what the other panelists were doing so I could have done the same.

Shelly W., Bellaire, Michigan

moderator talks

An even better opportunity to build your credibility in the field, as well as your company's, is to moderate a panel. Here your role is more of an organizer and facilitator than a participant, and as such you won't necessarily be expected to deliver commentary. Phew! However, you will need to be able to coach your panelists into a lively discussion with the audience. Think of being a moderator as being the host of a party.

Here's how it works. Your company is sponsoring a conference, and your boss has asked you to moderate a panel on a subject near and dear to your heart. You accept, of course. Next, you put on your organizational hat and pick panelists who will best explore the topic from their area of expertise. Once your panelists have accepted, you need to go over the subject of their talk. Most moderators ask their panelists to send in an outline of their talk. When you have all the outlines in, you can then coordinate the talks and figure who should go first, second, etc.

Ideally, you should meet with your panelists before you all go on so you can explain the lineup and the format of the panel. Cover the amount of time each has to speak, and how you want to handle questions and answers. (Most moderators hold questions until all the panelists have spoken.)

When it's showtime, start by welcoming the audience and introducing yourself. Give a quick overview of the theme of the panel, explaining why it is important, relevant, or timely. Introduce each panelist before he or she speaks rather than at the opening of the session. (This way the audience will remember the panelist's name and credentials, and his remarks.) You need to simply state his name, title, and the title of his talk.

As the talk goes on, watch the clock. Gently remind your panelists to finish up if they go over their allotted time, and remember, your role as moderator is to guide the discussion. Resist any urge to jump in with your opinion, though you can express it indirectly through your line of questioning.

TOP FIVE TIPS FOR MODERATING A PANEL

1

Prior to the session, familiarize yourself with any audiovisual devices that will be used to avoid any waste of time or embarrassment.

2

Make the meeting room comfortable, e.g., mention coffee if it's available, open windows if the room is too warm.

3

When the audience has settled in, announce the purpose of the panel and how the panelists are sure to enlighten them.

4

After all the panelists have spoken, engage the panelists in a friendly, informative discussion. Remember, you are the moderator, so keep your opinions to yourself.

5

End the session by consolidating the panelists' viewpoints, leaving the audience with one strong message.

Handling Questions and Answers

The moderator's role becomes especially important during the question-and-answer phase. (For more info on Q&A, see pages 56–57.) Here the moderator needs not only to field the questions but to direct them to the proper speaker. (As with any question-and-answer period, moderators need to repeat the question so all can hear.) If there are no questions, then the moderator should have one or two in order to generate others. The goal of any moderator is get the panelists interacting with each other and the audience.

leading a seminar

Be a leader for a day

The responsibilities of a seminar leader are many, as are the rewards. But to ensure a smooth-running, professional program, there are at least two to three months of planning and preparation in store. Your first job is to determine your goal, in other words, decide what your one overriding goal is for the outcome of the seminar. Is the goal to sell a product or services? Or is the goal to inform and/or instruct? To help you figure it out, assemble a committee of experts to advise you on your seminar goals and how best to meet them. Things to consider: How many speakers will you have? Will there be a panel discussion? And if so, who will moderate it? Be sure to vary the format of the program, e.g., speaker followed by a film, followed by a panel, followed by a coffee break. This will help keep your attendees' interest.

Next, you need to check logistics, and in some cases, you may need to set a budget. Do you need audiovisual equipment and staff to run it? Will there be refreshments? A number of costs are associated with running a seminar. Will you pay your speakers? Is there a fee for the room? There are also ways to recoup your costs, such as charging attendees an admission fee. You can also get creative with your budget planning. Considering selling the sponsorship of a coffee break or cocktail hour to a company that would love some exposure to the group you are gathering (but doesn't compete with you for business!).

A Note about Dates

Before you set the date of your event, make sure:

- it's not on or near a federal or state holiday.

- there isn't a similar program planned for the same date nearby that would compete with your event for attendees.

STEP BY STEP: SEMINAR CHECKLIST

1. Once you have an outline of the program, meet with staff at the facility where the seminar will be held.

2. Tour the room in which it will be held, and discuss all your needs: projection, food and beverages, sound, lighting, table setup, pens, pads, water, etc.

3. Put all your needs in writing. Most facilities will prepare a contract with all these items covered. Read the contract carefully before you sign.

4. To all speakers who will be speaking at the seminar: Send a letter to confirm the date, time, and place of the seminar, the goal of the program, the topic they will address, whether they will receive a fee, what their A/V needs are, and any hotel or travel arrangements. Request that they send you biographies and an abstract or hard copy of their talks, to be handed out to attendees.

5. Four to six weeks before the seminar, mail out invitations to attendees. Include registration information. As you receive registration forms, process them immediately so you have an accurate head count. Send a written confirmation (by e-mail or snail mail) that you've received their registration and send a map of the facility and driving directions.

6. Prepare a participant packet. Each attendee should receive a packet upon arrival that includes an agenda, a list of attendees, speakers' bios, a summary or hard copy of each speech, and an evaluation form.

7. Create a seminar evaluation form and ask your attendees to fill them out before they depart. After you read the suggestions, summarize the suggestions in a memo to file so that you can refer to them the next time you plan an event.

8. Send out notes of appreciation—not only to the speakers who participated but to the key contacts at the facility you used (A/V support, hotel management, etc.). Theirs is often a thankless job, and a note of appreciation is always welcome. Plus, they'll likely remember you the next time you use their facility!

now what do I do?

Answers to common questions

I speak very softly. I have to give a talk on a panel and I am worried no one will hear me. What should I do?

For starters, ask if there will be a microphone at the table. If there isn't one, ask the moderator if you can be given one. Even with a microphone, bad speech habits can wreck a talk. Here's a tip: Ask a friend or colleague to sit at the back of the room and have him give you a hand signal if he can't hear you. A simple thumbs-up for louder or thumbs-down for quieter will suffice.

I have to give a talk to youngsters. Should I do anything special?

Engage your audience in creative ways. Before the meeting, slip envelopes in discreet locations around the room, such as under chairs, centerpieces, or dishes. At a particular point in your presentation, ask audience members to open their envelopes, and have them stand and read aloud the question, riddle, or fact contained inside. The contents of the envelopes should complement your topic in a fun and interesting way.

How will I know that I've succeeded in persuading my audience?

The goal of a persuasive speech is to convince members of your audience to change their minds or to take an action. You can't know if you've really succeeded unless you track their attitudes or behaviors over time. However, you can poll your audience informally with a show of hands following your presentation, or more formally with a mailed survey a few days later. But remember, "You can bring a horse to water, but you can't make him drink." The most that you can do is deliver a powerful and effective argument. Your conclusion should clinch this argument, leaving the audience enlightened and willing to reconsider their previously held beliefs.

I was asked to moderate a panel at an important industry conference. It's a huge opportunity for me, but I'm concerned that I might lose control of the panel, since they are all senior to me. How do I tell them to finish if they go over their time limit?

What a terrific opportunity! Not only will it be good for your career, it will give you practice at controlling the time limit issue without being confrontational. Here's how: If you think your panelists are apt to talk beyond their allotted time, use a prop such as a large timer (either the kind with sand that times eggs or a speaker's timer, which uses green, yellow, and red lights to indicate time left). A large prop is not only visible to the panelists, but the audience will see it too. When the speaker's time is up, you will have the support of the entire room to turn the mike over to the next panelist.

 **OW WHERE DO I GO?!**

PUBLICATIONS

Marketing and Promoting Your Own Seminars and Workshops
by Fred Gleeck

Seminars: The Emotional Dynamic
by Frank Maselli

Seminar Selling: The Ultimate Resource Guide to Marketing Financial Services
by Paul Karasik

CHAPTER 7

Your audience

Know thy audience
Ease your fears and find out all you can 114

What does your audience expect?
Meet their needs 116

Will they like your presentation?
Test-drive your audience by rehearsing your talk 118

Will they be comfortable?
Make it as pleasant as possible 120

What is your audience saying?
Learn to read their signals 122

Now what do I do?
Answers to common questions 124

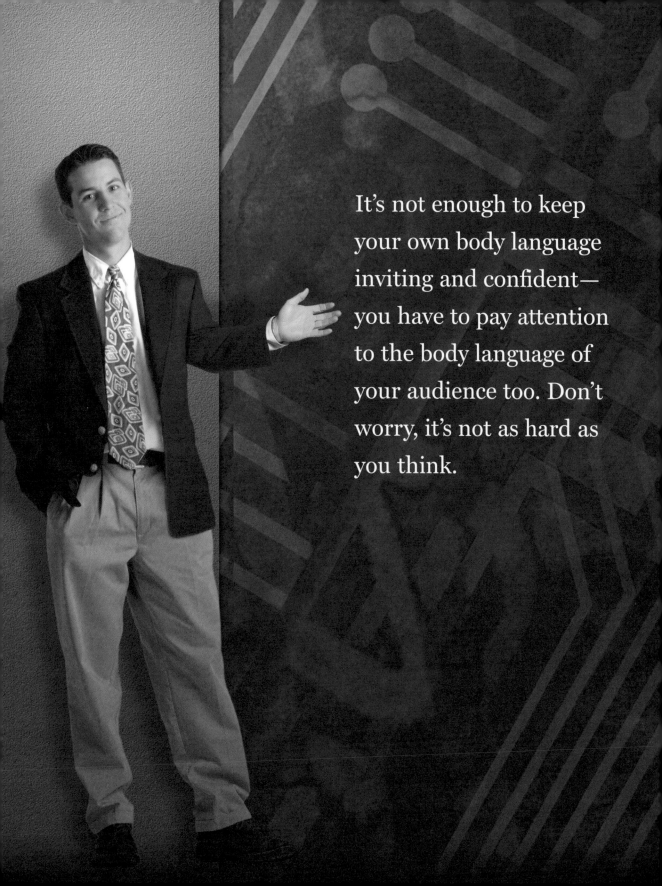

It's not enough to keep your own body language inviting and confident—you have to pay attention to the body language of your audience too. Don't worry, it's not as hard as you think.

know thy audience

Learn all you can about your listeners

To really communicate with your audience, learn everything you can about them ahead of time. Find out who your typical listener is. Friend or foe? Expert, familiar with, or totally clueless about your topic? What's the average age? How large is the group? Are different cultures, religions, or races represented? How many men and women will be present? Why are they there?

Understanding the motivation and background of your listeners will help you craft your presentation so that it makes the most sense to the most people. For example, is your audience there by choice? If so, they've already demonstrated that they have an interest in your topic. People whose attendance is required may not be as receptive to or interested in what you have to say, so you can prepare for that, perhaps by using more humor and less detail.

If your audience is small, you have an opportunity to get up close and personal. Take advantage of this valuable face time to score points by engaging your listeners, personalizing your talk, and involving them in the topic. It's harder for people in a small group to zone out during your talk, or yawn, nudge their buddy, or run out for coffee. With large audiences, learn what you can about areas of commonality. Are you all visiting Las Vegas for a conference? Comment about your first visit to the blackjack table or a curious sight you saw at a $1.95 buffet line. The trick is to build connections between you and your audience so they'll want to hear what you have to say.

ASK YOURSELF THESE QUESTIONS

- How many people will there be?

- What's the audience makeup? All men? Women and men? A mix of young and old? Why is my audience attending my talk?

- How well do they know my subject?

- Are they friend or foe? With me or against me?

- What am I trying to achieve with this audience?

ASK THE EXPERTS

I am speaking in front of 200 people! How can I connect with so many listeners?

Take everything you know about your audience, put it into a mental blender, and create a single living, breathing entity—an audience with one mind, heart, and belief system. If you strive to connect with that single entity, you'll feel as if you're communicating with just one person. It's much easier to address a large audience if you pretend it's one person. It allows you to be more personal and inclusive, and therefore more effective.

what does your audience expect?

Tell them what they want to hear

There's a Chinese proverb you'd do well to remember: Square words don't fit into a round ear. Let's say that you know why you've been invited to address your audience, and you know what you want to accomplish with your talk. You've researched who will attend your presentation, and you have a good idea of their background, experience, and level of interest in your topic. You know what you expect of them, but do you know what they expect of you?

It's simple. Audiences want their needs met. And the best way to meet their needs is to tell them what they want to hear. This doesn't mean that you should tell them something that they already know, agree with, or support. It means that whatever message you want to communicate must be communicated in such a way that meets their basic human needs so it becomes something that they want to hear.

For example, you are a tire manufacturer addressing an audience from the "Concerned Sport Utility Vehicle Owners of America." This could easily be a hostile group, with expectations that you'll dodge the tough issues about tire failure and SUVs. To get this group to really listen to you, you must be prepared to tackle the tough issues right off the bat. Then appeal to basic human needs such as security and esteem as discussed on page 101 by addressing advances made to ensure tire safety and how organizations such as theirs have brought these issues to the forefront and kept them there.

By meeting their needs head on, you'll exceed your audience's expectations as well as your own.

ASK THE EXPERTS

I'm well known for having a great sense of humor. I have to present to a group of people in my company, and I think my audience will expect me to be funny. Is humor appropriate for a corporate presentation?

What's appropriate is that you be yourself when you present to an audience. If you address your audience in a sober, dry, and deadly serious manner (which is completely different from how you present yourself from day to day), people will wonder what's wrong with you. Be yourself. (See pages 26–27 for tips on humor.)

FIRST PERSON DISASTER STORY

When in Rome, do as the Romans do

I own a chain of natural-food stores specializing in organic groceries and vitamins, and was invited to address an audience of people interested in franchise opportunities with my company. It was the dead of winter, and I wore a very professional-looking wool skirt suit with suede boots. As I took my place at the podium, I had all I could do to talk over the hoots and hollers in the audience. They were booing my boots! I had no idea that they would all be rabidly vegan, and totally anti-animal products. I learned an important lesson about giving presentations: Always find out who you are speaking to before you go onstage.

Jana H., Sheffield, Massachusetts

will they like your presentation?

Rehearse your talk
in front of a few
well-chosen listeners

Hollywood producers do it. Broadway show producers do it too. And you should as well—preview your work to a test audience before you go live.

Who do you get to listen to you? If it's a highly informational, technical talk that will be given to fellow techies, consider asking one or two people who are as expert on your topic as you are. As experts, they can point out any gaps in the information you provide, offer suggestions on improving the data and visuals you've selected, and help you improve the effectiveness of your argument.

If your talk is more general in nature, choose a few listeners who would be similar in makeup to the real listeners of your talk. Ask them to comment on your speech delivery and the flow of information. They can help you refine your presentation style and indicate where the flow of information doesn't make sense.

One rule of thumb about test audiences: They can't interrupt your talk. That's because you want your test presentation to be as close to your final talk as possible. Have them make notes for discussion after you've finished your rehearsal. And use this session to brainstorm about questions that you might get after your actual talk. You'll be able to formulate and rehearse your answers with your test group—a much more desirable scenario than being stumped for an answer in front of a hostile audience.

There's a reason those Hollywood and Broadway moguls believe in preview performances—they work!

GIVING CONSTRUCTIVE CRITICISM

Your test audience members might not know how to give constructive criticism, so you might want to set out these guidelines for their comments before rehearsing your talk.

Be specific Though it feels great when someone tells you they thought your talk was terrific, you need particulars. Your test audience can be more helpful to you by pointing out what specifically worked for them. Some examples of specific feedback: "I appreciated the engaging anecdote at the beginning," or "I felt there was a logical progression in your argument," or "I think the closing wrapped all your ideas together well."

Use "I" statements Audience test members should speak for themselves in describing how they perceived, reacted to, or understood what you said. Their comments should be "I" statements, not "you" statements. "I didn't understand your analogy to Plato" is good feedback; the person takes ownership of the confusion he or she felt. "Your analogy to Plato didn't make sense" is bad feedback: It assumes all listeners felt the same way.

Observe, don't judge Feedback should focus on what was observed, without any inferences drawn from the observation. For example, helpful feedback is, "I noticed that you didn't look up from your script very often." Judgmental feedback is, "It's obvious that you haven't practiced your speech very much, because you can't take your eyes off your script."

will they be comfortable?

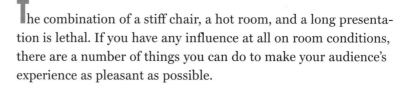

How to set the scene

The combination of a stiff chair, a hot room, and a long presentation is lethal. If you have any influence at all on room conditions, there are a number of things you can do to make your audience's experience as pleasant as possible.

Refreshments No one ever complained about having coffee and soft drinks available during a meeting. If possible, offer a beverage and snack table at the back of the room. Use paper cups and plates so there are no dishes clattering during your talk.

Sight lines You need to be visible to all the people in the room. In a large room, chairs should be set up theater-style, with aisles. Stagger the chairs so that people don't sit directly in front of each other. If the room is huge, consider projecting your image on a large screen behind you when you aren't showing visuals. Or use a video camera hooked up to TVs placed toward the back third of the room.

Temperature A setting of 68 degrees is ideal. Remember, rooms warm up as they fill with people and stage lights and computer equipment are turned on. While it may be hard to guesstimate what your initial temperature setting should be, it's better to err on the side of being too cool. It helps keep people alert.

Podium If you are speaking from a podium, be sure you can be seen. If the podium is as tall as you are, your audience will get distracted and ultimately disinterested if they can't see you. Consider working from a lower, transparent, or tabletop podium instead.

Stage set Make the stage as attractive as possible. Have banners, flags, or other signs appropriate to the event. All these added visuals offer eye relief to the audience.

Sound Make sure you can be heard in all four corners of the room. Refine your microphone technique during your rehearsal. Make sure you don't turn away from the microphone as you speak. Practice how close your lips can get to the mike without "popping" your p's or "hissing" your s's.

ASK THE EXPERTS

I have to give a long speech at the end of the day, and there is no budget for coffee or snacks. What can I do?

If there's no money in the budget, then consider bringing in a few boxes of cookies and a carafe of water. Your audience will appreciate your thoughtfulness.

I've noticed that people like to sit in the back of the room, especially if it's a talk I have to give and they have to listen to. Should I take their seat placement personally?

People who sit in the back can be signaling their lack of interest. Feel free to ask your audience to move closer to you. By having them closer, you can create a more intimate atmosphere and engage their attention more easily.

what is your audience saying?

If they snooze, you lose!

That's right. It's not enough to keep your own body language inviting and confident, but you have to pay attention to the body language of your audience, too. Don't worry, it's not as hard as you think. Fortunately, your audience is in a constant state of communication, so it is fairly easy to monitor their reaction and adapt accordingly.

Here are some audience reactions that every speaker loves:

- leaning forward intently
- nodding in agreement
- taking notes
- smiling warmly
- meeting your eye contact
- clapping
- laughing

Here's what you don't want to see your audience doing:

- yawning
- nodding out
- fidgeting
- smiling in a frozen way
- squinting at you
- avoiding your eye contact
- crossing their arms and legs
- talking
- stretching
- tapping their feet

Be sensitive to your audience's reactions. There are so many reasons to make sure that you are connecting with them, besides ensuring that your talk is a smash hit. You'll build credibility for yourself, support for your project, and a foundation of respect to enhance your reputation. An added bonus: You'll probably get fewer questions or requests to clarify points you've already made!

STEP BY STEP: GETTING BACK ON TRACK

Here are some ideas to get a confused, bored, or distracted audience back on track:

1. If someone looks puzzled, stop your talk and ask them if they are.

2. Move around the room.

3. Use emphasis in your voice.

4. Don't repeat yourself.

5. Use language that's specific and clear.

6. Use silence to get attention.

7. Slow down! It may be that you're talking too fast.

8. Finish each idea before proceeding to the next.

A Relevant Quote

"A yawn is a silent shout."
—Gilbert Keith Chesterton, English poet

now what do I do?

Answers to common questions

I have to give a talk to a group of people who I know don't share the same views that I do. What should I do?

The trick to dealing with a so-called "hostile" audience is to be open-minded. That means giving a speech that is balanced and respectful of their opinions.

Should I vary my speech based on whether I am talking to a large group or a small one?

Yes, you should, and here are the reasons why. In a small group (say 15 or less), the odds are that the members of the audience know each other. They will not want to appear as if they are daydreaming nor be caught off guard. Be sure to give this audience solid, reasonable information that they want to hear. In a large audience where the members are not known to each other, you need to be more dramatic to wake up the daydreamers. The larger the audience, the more of a show you will need to put on.

I want to be sure I know who I am addressing. How do I get information about my audience?

Good question. For starters, ask the person who invited you to speak about the makeup of your audience. Then see if you can talk with someone who will actually be in the audience. Ask that person what he thinks his group wants to hear and why. It's also a good idea to know what is currently going on with your audience. If it's an organization or company, contact their public relations department; if it's a municipality, see if there is anything in the local newspaper about recent issues.

I want to use some humor in my presentation, but I am afraid it will backfire. How do you use humor effectively?

Humor is a wonderful tool to enliven a presentation. But it must be used sparingly. The trick to using humor is to turn its edge on you, the speaker, and not the audience. In other words, use humor to make fun of yourself, but not others. You should bear the brunt of your jokes, not the audience.

What happens if an audience member starts to heckle me?

Fortunately, you would have done research on your audience prior to your talk to get a sense of whether your listeners will be friend or foe. If you expect that you might be heckled, remember that you don't want to give the heckler a victory by losing your composure. Often hecklers are simply hushed down by people sitting around them or escorted out before you get a chance to address their challenge. But if their disruption is allowed to continue, look directly at the person and briefly respond. You can offer to discuss the issue after your talk is completed. If this doesn't help, ask to have the person removed.

I have to give a talk to a group of our international marketing arm. The problem is that they are all coming in from overseas and I am worried they will be too tired to listen. What should I do?

You are right to be concerned. If you fear that jet lag may get the better of your audience, then address that concern right up front. Tell your audience that you appreciate the fatigue they might be experiencing—this immediately builds trust. If you can, tell them that you have pared down your talk to the essentials and that those who are interested can stay after your talk to ask questions.

OW WHERE DO I GO?!

CONTACTS	PUBLICATIONS
www.presentations.com	**Speak Smart** by Thomas Mira
www.executive-speaker.com	
	Great Presentation Skills by Melody Templeton and Suzanne Fitzgerald

CHAPTER 8

Using visuals

The power of visual aids
What they can and can't do **128**

Setting the scene
Choose the right visual support option
for your meeting **130**

35mm slides
State-of-the-art visuals for the power
presentation **132**

Presentation software
Make your slides yourself **134**

Videotape
A great pace breaker for long talks **136**

Overhead transparencies
Use overhead charts for both formal
and informal presentations **138**

Flip charts
How you can use flip charts to promote
audience interaction **140**

Handouts
The good, the bad, and the ugly **142**

Tools of the trade
The pros and cons of each **144**

Now what do I do?
Answers to common questions **146**

Before you start stressing over what kinds of visual aids you might want, relax and take a moment to think. What do you want your visual aid to do? Aid. Exactly. Whatever visual support you choose, remember that the operative word is "support." Slides, overheads, video, audio, computer-generated presentations, or flip charts should support and enhance your message, not duplicate or dominate it.

the power of visual aids

An image can be worth a thousand words

The right choice of visual aid can help you bring your presentation to life, often more effectively and memorably than words alone. Again, the reason for this is the power of the eye over the ear. Visual aids usually pack a more memorable impact than words. For instance, telling an audience that profits are up 45% is one thing, but illustrating that figure with a graphic of a large arrow sweeping upward really brings home the good news.

Before you start stressing over what kinds of visual aids you might want, relax and take a moment to think. What do you want your visual aid to do? Aid. Exactly. Whatever visual support you choose, remember that the operative word is "support." Slides, overheads, video, audio, computer-generated presentations, or flip charts should support and enhance your message, not duplicate or dominate it. Use them only to add color and life to the points you make.

The pages to follow will describe the pros and cons of the many visual aids available to you. And you'll learn how to prepare yourself for, and recover gracefully from, the inevitable brush with one of Murphy's unwritten laws: If you can plug it in, it will break.

ASK THE EXPERTS

Can't I just rely on my words to communicate my message?

Of course you can. But if you want your audience to remember what you said, visual aids are the way to go. Studies show that audiences have memories like sieves: They retain only about 20% of what they hear and 30% of what they see. But they will remember about 50% of what they hear *and* see. Visual aids will not only help make your presentation more memorable, they can dramatize and clarify your points.

What if I can't talk and operate a slide projector at the same time?

A lot of speakers are concerned about losing their place in their 35mm or PowerPoint slides, or getting lost in a sea of acetate transparencies. You have a few options here. First, practice until you know every slide by heart, so if you advance too many times (or not enough), you should know exactly what's in front of or behind the slide that's being projected. Second, mark your script (see page 162) so that a miniature of the correct slide appears alongside your script. You'll know by glancing at the screen whether the slide matches what you're saying. If it doesn't, use your marked script as a guide to get you to the correct slide. Finally, enlist an assistant to advance your slides or transparencies for you, but make sure you practice together ahead of time till you are both comfortable with the sequence and flow.

VISUAL PERSUADERS

In 1986 the 3M Corporation commissioned a study on the power of presentation slides. They found that presenters who used visual aids were 43% more effective in persuading audience members to take a specific course of action than presenters who didn't use visuals.

setting the scene

The tools you use—whether they are simple props to reinforce an idea or electronic audiovisual devices—should be carefully thought out so that they are appropriate, relevant, and visible. Here are some questions to help frame your choices:

Are they appropriate? Think about your audience. If it's an informal gathering of salespeople, using props, slides, or video as motivational tools could be very effective. If it's a small, formal gathering of senior executives, you may want to get to the point quickly with a crisp, professional PowerPoint presentation.

Are they relevant? Think about your speech. Your visuals should support your words, not the other way around. No matter how magnificent your slide of sunrise over the Himalayas or birds flying in formation, if it doesn't complement and enhance your topic, then it doesn't belong in your presentation.

Are they visible? Think about the room. If there are windows without blinds, a video or slides might be washed out by the daylight. And be sure to do your homework ahead of time on the room setup. Theater-style, U-shaped, or classroom seating all dictate where you should stand to make your visual aids work to your advantage.

WORKING WITH DIFFERENT ROOM ARRANGEMENTS

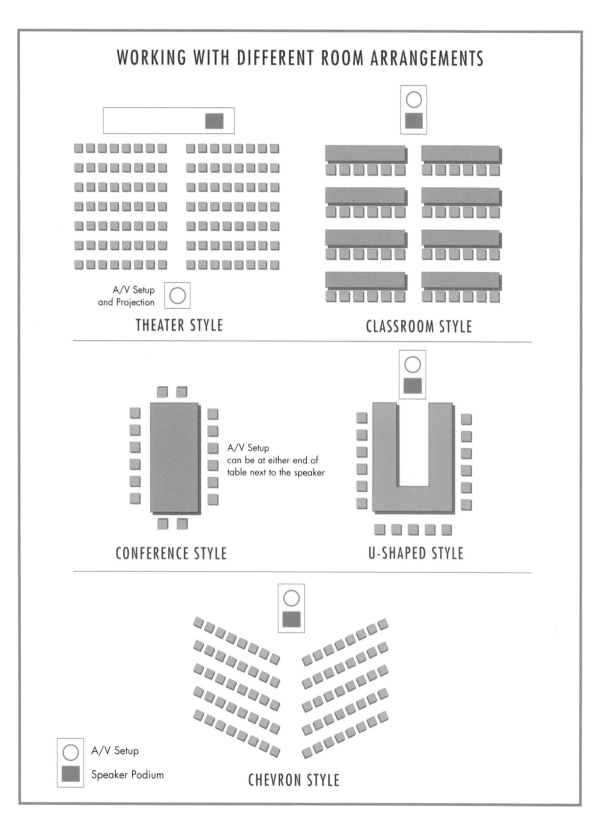

A/V Setup and Projection

THEATER STYLE

CLASSROOM STYLE

A/V Setup can be at either end of table next to the speaker

CONFERENCE STYLE

U-SHAPED STYLE

A/V Setup

Speaker Podium

CHEVRON STYLE

35mm slides

The best visual for the big screen

Okay, you have to give a presentation to your entire division. That's 300 people. You've gotten over your panic and poured your nervous energy into researching and writing your speech. You've even rehearsed it, complete with deep-breathing exercises. But it could use a bit of a visual impact, especially since you will need to discuss a few technical points that could so easily be shown in a few charts and graphs. What to do? You can't really give out hand-outs—the group is too large for that. Ask around (try the head of facilities) and see if there is a screen in the room in which you are to speak. Could you project computer-generated slides on the screen? Yes, but the room and screen are too large for computer-formatted images. The images would blur and be hard to read.

You need to project charts and graphs so that they are crystal clear and rich in color. You need 35mm slides. Nothing compares with the clarity of image and density of color, and the image quality is as excellent projected on a small screen or a super-size one. There are a number of ways to create presentations with 35mm slides. Perhaps the easiest, and alas, most costly, is to hire a company that's equipped to design and produce these slides. Your job is simply to provide the text and graphs you want included, and the firm will design the slides, using colors and a format you approve. You'll be given a hard copy of the final presentation to review. Once you've made your edits, the firm will convert the file to 35mm slides. Just look in your yellow pages under "Computer Graphics and Imaging," or "Digital Imaging" to find providers in your area.

35mm slide projector

If you are more adventurous (or on a tight budget) you can create your own slides using one of many presentation software programs available (see page 134). Once you have created the slides on your computer, you can send them electronically to an imaging company to have them converted to 35mm slides. You save money on design, but still get the same high-quality image you want that signals a professional presentation.

ASK THE EXPERTS

I'd like to use 35mm slides in my presentation. Should I clear the expense with my boss?

Clearing expenses with your boss is always a good idea. Slide costs vary dramatically, however, depending on how fast you need them and how much of the work you are willing to do. If you use a digital imaging company to design and produce the slide, you can expect to spend around $50 per hour of their time. If you have a lot of edits, those costs can add up. And if you need the slides on a 3-hour turnaround, it could run you $150 per slide. On the other hand, if you design the slides on your own computer using presentation software, send the file electronically or by disk to the imaging company, and give them a 3-day turnaround, your costs could be as low as $4 or $5 per slide.

How should I go about getting slides created?

If you work for a medium-to-large company, it's always smart to talk to the professionals in your communications department. If they can't produce the slides for you, they can direct you to companies who can. Plus, your company may have graphic standards that serve as guidelines for logo usage and creation of all marketing materials. Many companies want a consistent look to their external communications vehicles, and slides certainly fall into that category. Your communications department staff will be well versed in these guidelines.

Should I practice with the slide projector before I give my presentation?

Yes! A technical run-through is key to a successful presentation. First, if you are operating the slides using a remote-control clicker, then set aside some time to stage a run-through. If a technical assistant will be operating the projector for you, then provide him or her with a marked-up copy of your presentation; note where slide A, B, and C, etc. are to be flashed.

---

presentation software

It's easier to use than you think

What was the business world like before presentation software programs arrived on the scene? Was it all black and white and boring, with no zing, pizzazz, or zest? Hardly. But the advent of powerful software progams that enable even the most timid technophobe to create professional-looking presentations has truly changed the face of business meetings forever.

Presentation software, such as Microsoft PowerPoint, allows you to design "slides" on your computer complete with spiffy-looking

type, charts, graphs, illustration, animation, photography, or even a live link to the Internet. You can select from predesigned formats (called templates), choose cool-looking background patterns, and experiment with color. Moreover, your presentation can be updated instantly, carried with you on trips, posted on the Web, e-mailed to prospective clients, displayed on a laptop, or projected on the side of a building. (See chapter 9 to learn how to operate PowerPoint like a pro.)

But flexibility, portability, and ease of use have also made computer-generated slide shows as ubiquitous and poorly executed as prune danish at a Monday morning staff meeting. Far too many over-designed, word-heavy, and inconsistently formatted slides have led to a backlash against this wildly popular presentation tool, and in some circles, it is considered a plague. Despite the recent backlash, computer-generated slides can be an extraordinarily effective way to get and hold your audience's attention while you build your credibility.

ASK THE EXPERTS

Are there any quick ways to learn just the basic features of different presentation software packages?

You can go to **www.About.com** and type in "Presentation software" in the "Find It Now" box. You'll have access to online tutorials, articles, tips, and free software downloads. Be forewarned about free downloads, however, as they frequently are not fully tested, nor do they offer the high level of customer support and program documentation you would get from a more commercially available product. Turn to chapter 9 for a step-by-step guide to creating slides on PowerPoint.

I have to give a presentation to a large group. Can I use my PowerPoint in a large room?

Here's the rub: In most cases, running a PowerPoint presentation on your laptop or projecting it directly onto a wall or screen works just fine. But if you are presenting to a large (or especially important) audience, and your slides are fairly complex or need to be projected large to be seen, inevitably image deterioration occurs. Wavy lines and washed-out colors are common. One way to remedy this situation is to send the presentation you created in PowerPoint to an imaging company, and they can create 35mm slides (see page 132) from your file. You can send your presentation electronically or express mail a floppy disk and get your slides there the next day. What you lose in flexibility (it's not as easy to make last-minute edits to your presentation) you gain in quality. Nothing compares with 35mm slides for color saturation or image clarity.

videotape

Next to coffee breaks, business videos rank high on the audience relief scale

A videotape can be a welcome relief for your audience, particularly if your presentation is long, or you are one of many on a long list of presenters. To use a videotape as a visual aid, you first need to have the time and budget to produce a tape prior to your talk that focuses on a specific aspect of your presentation (i.e., a plant tour, a product launch). But if you don't have either time or money, there are many business videos that can be rented or purchased.

For example, if you are giving a talk on overcoming obstacles, you might want to open your presentation with an exciting 2-minute video of people driven to new heights of achievement in extreme sports. For a talk on change management, you could run a fun, short video based on the best-selling book by Spencer Johnson, "Who Moved My Cheese?" If you are looking for a bit of humor, try John Cleese of Monty Python fame. He has a series of hilarious tapes on topics ranging from handling demanding customers to serving the client after the sale.

Be sure to determine ahead of time that the video you choose is both relevant to your talk and appropriate to your audience. But whatever tape you show, you can be sure your audience will appreciate the change in pace it provides.

ASK THE EXPERTS

What should I do if something happens to the video projector and I can't show my tape?

It's always a good idea to have a plan for continuing your presentation without the benefit of your visual aids. If your equipment fails, don't spend more than 2 or 3 minutes trying to fix the problem—longer than that will alienate your audience. And don't apologize; just explain gracefully (or with good humor) that technical problems prevent you from showing your video. Then get on with the show, like the pro that you are.

There's a 2-minute segment in a James Bond film that would work perfectly for a sales pitch I plan to give. How can I get a good quality clip of it?

In short, you can't. Commercial films are protected by strict copyright laws, and any use outside of the normal rental for personal viewing is forbidden. Besides being illegal, using a segment from a commercial film is risky. What you consider funny could be viewed by audience members as offensive. Use the video resources listed here, or research others on the Internet. These videos are designed for business audiences, and many here are clever, effective, and inspiring.

VIDEO SHOW BASICS

Familiarize yourself with the video equipment.

Make sure your tape is rewound and cued to the right spot.

Use two or three monitors, or one large projection screen, to ensure that everyone can see your video.

Check sound levels and color balance before you present.

If you can, bring a spare tape.

SOURCES FOR PRE-PRODUCED BUSINESS VIDEOS

Here are just three of many suppliers of business videos. Visit their Web sites to order a catalogue or view free previews.

Enterprise Media LLC
Phone: 1-800-423-6021
E-mail: stewart@enterprisemedia.com
Web site: **www.enterprisemedia.com**

CRM Learning
Phone: 1-800-421-0833
E-Mail: sales@crmlearning.com
Web site: **www.crmfilms.com**

McKay Training Videos
Phone: 1-888-281-8038
E-mail: questions@trainingabc.com
Web site:
www.mckaytrainingvideos.com

overhead transparencies

Sometimes old technology communicates a refreshing new commitment

Overhead projectors are as old as the hills. You remember them from high school, college, and training sessions early in your career: the whirring fan, fidgeting to focus the image, and the inevitable keystone 'wedge,' where the top part of the image is much wider than the bottom.

Of course, things have changed a lot since then. Projectors have gotten brighter and quieter, and the transparencies you use can be made to look very professional. What has stayed the same, though, is the persona that this very low-tech system seems to have—a sort of "roll up your sleeves, we're getting down to business" quality. And best of all, you can do them yourself quickly and easily. Of course, it helps if you have good handwriting.

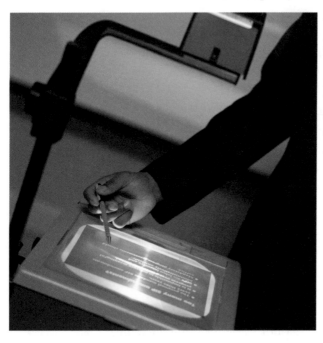

With the right attitude and preparation, you can capture this same no-nonsense yet audience-engaging delivery during your presentation. Overhead projectors are perfect vehicles for getting close to your audience and inviting their participation, and they prove that you don't need the latest technology to make the biggest impact.

Overhead Projector Tool Kit

Spare bulbs

Extension cord

Alcohol wet-nap (to wipe off projector lens)

Extra colored markers

Spare blank transparencies

Duct tape (to tape down the electrical cord)

KEEP THESE TIPS IN MIND

- Use cardboard frames for each transparency.

- Write your key points on the frames.

- Sequentially number the frames.

- Keep text to a minimum—your transparencies should support your talk, not duplicate it.

- Make sure the audience's sight lines are clear.

- Rest a pen or pencil on the transparency to use as a pointer.

- Use bright markers to circle key words on your transparencies as you speak. You'll convey enthusiasm for your topic and focus your audience to the main points.

- Reveal information by covering part of your transparency with an opaque sheet of paper. Even better: Create multiple transparencies with bullet points that "build" on each other.

- Turn the projector off between transparencies if you plan to talk for more than a few minutes.

FIRST PERSON   DISASTER STORY

The Migraine Presentation

I'll never forget the sinking feeling I had when at the end of an all-day meeting, the last presenter arrived with a 2-inch stack of overheads. He flipped on the machine and started riffling through his transparencies, tossing every other one aside and mumbling, "Nope . . . not that one . . . that's not it . . ." as if he'd never seen them before. The whole time between transparencies he left the projector on, causing a blinding white light on the screen. He put every one down backwards, then looked up at the screen, then back to the transparency, then flipped it over and read everything line for line. I thought I would go insane, until he finally finished, scooped up his sheets, and walked out, but not before tripping over the wire and pulling the projector plug out of the wall.

Vince L., Wayne, New Jersey

flip charts

A quick and easy communications tool

Of all the visual aids available to you, flip charts can be the most informal, interactive, and inexpensive means of communicating with your audience. And the most low-tech: just some large pads of paper mounted to an easel and a few colored markers. No dimming of lights, no out-of-focus slides, no remote mouse—not even an electrical outlet to be concerned about.

But even a simple flip-chart presentation requires a great deal of pre-talk planning. First, consider the size of your group. Flip charts work best in smaller rooms with audiences of 50 people or fewer. Then, decide how you want to use the charts. You have several options for presenting information, which can be combined depending on the objectives of your talk. For example:

- Draw your charts ahead of time. Simply turn the pages as you speak.

- Lightly pencil in your charts ahead of time. Then go over your pencil lines (which won't be visible to your audience) with a marker as you speak.

- Write your charts as you speak. A more casual approach (and more likely to be, well, messy).

- If your goal is to present your talk and then solicit ideas from your audience, consider having two flip charts. Use one for your talking points, and use the other to jot down ideas from your group members. Consider asking someone from your audience to serve as scribe.

- Flip charts are super for budget-conscious presenters as well as facilitators seeking group feedback. Used wisely, flip chart presentations can leave your audience with a sense of having been involved in your talk and of having contributed to its outcome.

ⒶSK THE EXPERTS

I know my talk is going to generate lots of ideas from my audience. How do I keep control of my presentation?

As much as your audience will want to participate, it's still your show. The way to keep control is to exert it. When you feel your audience has generated enough ideas on a topic, ask them to now choose the top five or ten ideas and write them on a clean chart. Continue this way—generate lots of comments and then get the group's consensus on the top five or ten—to narrow down the lists and build group support for the top ideas. At the end of your presentation, you'll have a manageable number of ideas which you can then assemble into a report and send to all the meeting participants a week or so after your presentation. Remember, you are in charge of your presentation, and you can tighten the reins at any time if you feel you are losing control.

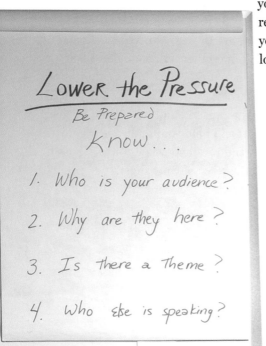

handouts

Speakers hate them, but audiences love them!

Next to delivering the speech itself, few things cause presenters more needless angst than the issue of handouts. Questions abound: Should I distribute them? If yes, should I do it before or after my presentation? What if everyone focuses on the handout and doesn't pay attention to me? What if they ask questions about material I haven't covered yet? And if they read ahead to my conclusions, won't that screw up the case I'm trying to build?

The truth is, you have to accept that all of these scenarios could happen. But handouts are a winning proposition if you are willing to accept that your job is not to control your audience members, but rather to do everything you can to assist them in understanding and retaining the very compelling presentation that you are about to give. Handouts are designed to meet their needs, not yours.

This is a good time to remember that your presentation is not about YOU—how glib or entertaining you are—it is about your communicating a topic effectively to a group of people. The most successful presentations are those that persuade an audience to a different viewpoint, open their minds to new ideas, or leave them fully briefed on a situation where information was lacking before. You can't control how your audience will absorb or react to the information you present, and you should let go of any desire to do so. Handouts will help your audience members follow your thought process and recall your key points. These two results alone are worth the price of your angst!

TWO GOLDEN RULES

If you distribute copies of your visual aids (overheads, slides, or PowerPoint presentation), do so before you speak. That way audience members will have something to follow along with and take notes on.

If you distribute copies of your speech, or an outline of it, do so after your presentation has concluded. You can leave copies on a table at the back of the room. Just let your audience know that they can pick up a copy after the session is over.

DESIGN YOUR HANDOUTS FOR MAXIMUM IMPACT

Today's presentation software allows you to print up to 12 slides per page. Two or three slides per page are probably the most effective format, because they are highly legible and leave plenty of room for your audience to take notes.

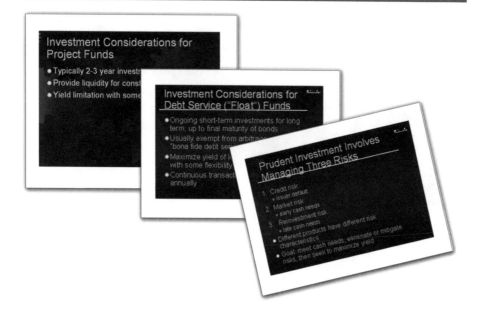

tools of the trade

To do the job right,
choose the right tool

You're only limited by your creativity when it comes to conceptualizing and producing visual aids to support your presentation. The pros and cons of some popular options are described here.

35mm Slides

Text, graphics, and photography composed on 35mm slides.
Pros: Brilliant, saturated color. Excellent legibility even in the largest of rooms.
Cons: Expense. Though often designed in-house on presentation software, they must be sent by disk or via e-mail to an imaging company to be turned into 35mm slides. Depending on complexity and rush, costs can run from $3 to $35 per slide.
Best used for: Large rooms arranged theater-style.

PowerPoint Presentation Software

Computer generated "slides" projected on laptop or large screen (see chapter 9).
Pros: Inexpensive, after the initial cost of software. Flexible, able to edit up until the last minute before speech. Easy to create, even by high-tech neophytes.
Cons: In large rooms, projected image can be washed-out and hard to read.
Best used for: Small to midsize groups.

Videotape

Can be produced specifically for your speech or rented through stock video houses (see page 136).
Pros: Can be great relief for audience.
Cons: Can be expensive to rent or create.
Best used for: Works well in all sizes of groups and room settings.

Overheads

Text or graphics on transparent acetate, projected on a screen.
Pros: Inexpensive, easy to update.
Cons: Acetates are tricky to handle. Projector looks like ancient technology.
Best used for: Small to midsize groups.

Flip Charts

Large pads of grid paper on easels.
Pros: Inexpensive, can be highly interactive, great for brainstorming sessions.
Cons: Conclusions must be captured and distributed after session is over.
Best used for: Small group meetings.

Handouts

Key points from your presentation printed up and distributed to audience.
Pros: Reinforces your key messages.
Cons: There's an art to timing when your handouts are distributed (see page 142). People may read ahead and not focus on you.
Best used for: Works well for all sizes of groups and room settings.

Props

Objects displayed or passed around to illustrate a point.
Pros: Makes your point memorable, "up close and personal."
Cons: If people hang on to the object too long, others may miss the point.
Best used for: Small and midsize group meetings.

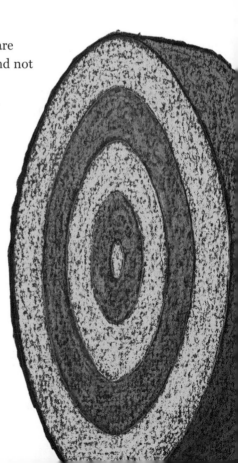

now what do I do?

Answers to common questions

I'm thinking of using either 35mm slides or PowerPoint. Should the room be completely dark for the audience to better view my visual aids?

No. In fact, you do your audience a disservice by completely darkening the room. Leave enough light for them to comfortably take notes or find their way out of the room if they must leave. Besides, a dark room almost guarantees that someone will nod off.

I have to give a presentation to a client on our company's third-quarter results, which were dreadful. Any suggestions on how to communicate these numbers visually?

Bad results are best communicated in table form. A series of numbers across the page will do less damage viscerally than a bar chart or line graph of the same information.

Bad news presented the wrong way

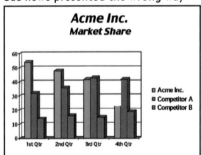

Bad news presented the right way

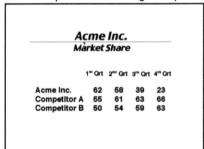

Conversely, positive results should be represented graphically, using bar charts or line graphs that reinforce the good news visually.

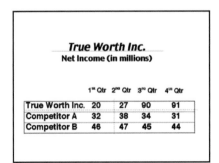

Good news presented badly

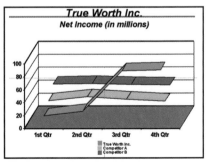

Good news presented well

What can I do if my equipment fails?

Remember the Boy Scouts' motto: Be prepared. It's been said that the latest computerized presentation and projection systems are truly intelligent systems. In fact, they are so smart they know exactly when you are about to begin to speak, and then they break down.

If all goes black, don't spend more than a minute or two trying to fix the problem, at the risk of alienating your audience. Keep the attitude that the show must go on. The difference is that you will read aloud the main points that would have appeared on the screen if the systems hadn't failed. (Normally, you would simply comment on the projected text and NEVER read what appears word for word—your audience knows how to read.) Your quick recovery in a difficult situation such as this demonstrates to your audience what a pro you are.

What's the best way to use a pointer?

Pointers are a bit tricky. Laser pointers look very *Star Trek* and are difficult to hold steady. If you have even the slightest case of jitters, they aren't recommended. Wooden pointers can send some audience members time-tripping back to grammar school. There are telescopic metal pointers that strike a balance between the past and the future, but generally, if you can avoid using a pointer, do so. You shouldn't have so many elements on each slide that you'd need to single them out individually.

NOW WHERE DO I GO?!

CONTACTS	PUBLICATIONS
Some of the more popular presentation software packages include:	**Present Yourself!** By Michael J. Gelb
Microsoft PowerPoint: www.microsoft.com/office/powerpoint	
Adobe Photoshop: www.adobe.com/products/photoshop/main.html	

CHAPTER 9

PowerPoint power

What is PowerPoint?
Do-it-yourself presentation **150**

Starting
How to begin **152**

AutoContent outlines
Over 30 outlines to choose from **154**

Meet PowerPoint
The anatomy of a slide **156**

Editing presentations
Putting it in your own words **158**

Using design templates
How to slick up the look of your work **160**

Other PowerPoint features
Cool tools you can use **162**

New views on your slides
Manipulate your view of the slides **164**

Transitions
Going from one slide to the next **166**

Build slides
High-tech transitions **168**

Using blank presentations
Doing it from scratch **170**

Printing and presenting
Making user-friendly handouts **172**

Tips for using slides
Smart things to do **174**

Now what do I do?
Answers to common questions **176**

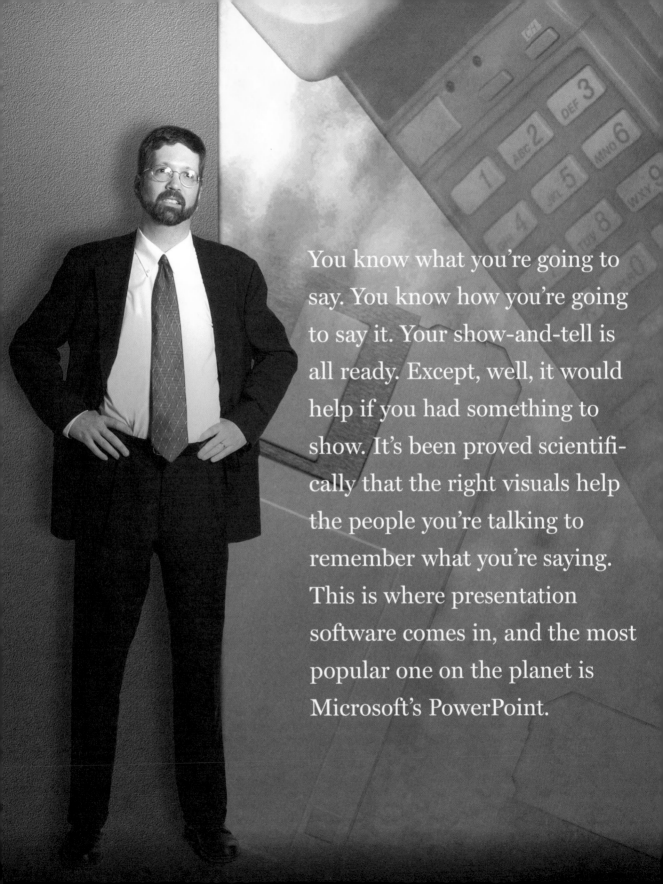

You know what you're going to say. You know how you're going to say it. Your show-and-tell is all ready. Except, well, it would help if you had something to show. It's been proved scientifically that the right visuals help the people you're talking to remember what you're saying. This is where presentation software comes in, and the most popular one on the planet is Microsoft's PowerPoint.

what is PowerPoint?

Professional presentations in the click of a mouse

It can be time-consuming as well as expensive to get photo-ready art and graphics for your presentation and then have an outside service bureau or corporate graphics department convert it into a slide presentation for you. And if some facts changed or you saw a mistake in your presentation after it was produced, you'd be charged an outrageous rush-job fee to correct your existing slides.

Fortunately, there is another way to jazz up your presentation. Use PowerPoint presentation software by Microsoft. Since it first came out in 1987, PowerPoint has become almost as ubiquitous in offices as Post-it notes and coffee cups. And there are good reasons for its popularity.

First of all, you control the look and words of the slides, so you can change them in an instant. Moreover, PowerPoint slides are highly portable. They can be stored and displayed on a laptop for a one-to-one meeting or projected onto a screen to an audience of over 100 people. PowerPoint is inexpensive too. If you give a lot of presentations, it's far less expensive than having 35mm slides created. And finally, PowerPoint software offers a host of images and slide formats to jazz up your presentation, and allows you to create handouts, talking points, and outlines in addition to slides.

It is so easy to use. Just click in each box and type in your own title and subtitle.

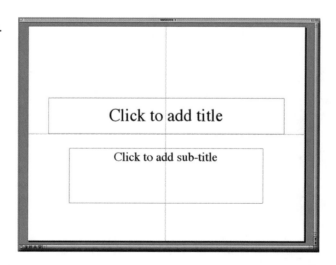

150

A SK THE EXPERTS

Where can I get PowerPoint?

You may already have it! For years, Microsoft included PowerPoint as part of its Microsoft Office Professional and Premium package for Windows PCs and the Mac. If you have Microsoft Office Professional or Premium on your computer, check the Office folder to see whether PowerPoint is already installed there. If it's not there, reinsert your Office setup CD and see whether it's there but was never installed. However, bear in mind that Microsoft is getting "creative" in its packaging of software, so it may have left PowerPoint off the version you have. If so, you may have to go out and buy a copy. It's available at most computer and office supply stores. The latest version (PowerPoint 2002 for Windows and PowerPoint 2001 for the Mac) costs around $200. (Or see if you can get a better deal buying it as part of the Microsoft Office package).

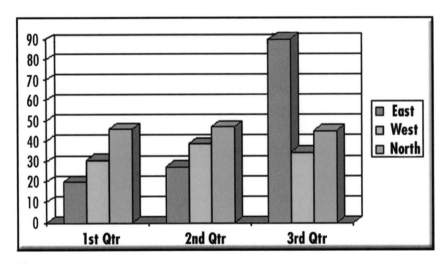

Here is a sample from PowerPoint's chart library. You can easily change the type, calibrations, and even the colors.

starting

Need an outline? Let the AutoContent Wizard create one for you

Great, you've thought through your ideas, and you've got a pile of notes ready to be converted into a smart, sleek presentation. Now you are ready to turn on that PowerPoint. Except you don't know where it is. Fine. No problem. Look in your applications folder (in Windows, this folder is under the Start menu's Programs or All Programs link).

Okay, now you are ready to begin. The first window you see will ask you what you want to use to create your new presentation. Huh? Don't panic. What this means is that you get a choice to either create it using a prepackaged outline (**AutoContent Wizard**), refine the look of your presentation after you have created it (**Design Template** or **Template**), or create your own presentation from scratch (**Blank Presentation**). Note: If Office Assistant pops up, you can close its window by clicking on the tiny box in the upper left-hand corner.

The easiest way to begin is with the AutoContent Wizard, where there are different outlines covering over 30 basic business presentations, such as Managing Organizational Change, Marketing Plan, or Financial Overview. Each outline contains between 4 and 12 slides. For example, if you have to give a talk on your company's latest reorganization, you would choose the Managing Organizational Change outline and let PowerPoint walk you through each of the 12 slides, from your opening remarks to your closing.

Click on AutoContent Wizard and let PowerPoint do the hard work for you.

STEP BY STEP: USING AUTOCONTENT WIZARD

1. After you start up PowerPoint, select the AutoContent Wizard button from the text box that appears and click OK.

2. In the Wizard box, browse the list for presentation **types** that suit your needs. Click the All button to see a list of all the outlines. Or search the outlines by category. Choose from General, Corporate, Projects, Sales/Marketing, and Carnegie Coach. (For more on these categories, see the next page.) Then click on the Next button.

3. The next step asks how you will present the slides. Are you going to be showing them to your audience on a projector screen, on the Web, as overhead slides, or 35mm slides? Pick the appropriate **style**, and click on the Next button.

4. Give your presentation a name, and then type in the date and slide number. Click Next again.

5. Finally, click the Finish button.

6. Depending on which outline you've chosen, the AutoContent Wizard will now take you step-by-step through your presentation. Use the down arrow key to move you through the steps. After you finish each slide, click OK and another prompt will pop up.

7. Once you are done, you can preview your presentation.

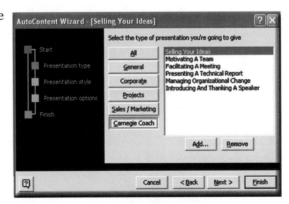

Here is the list of the six outlines that you will find under the Carnegie Coach category. (The black pane on the left tells you where you are in the Wizard process.)

AutoContent outlines

Don't be shy about experimenting with the different outlines that you'll find in the AutoContent Wizard. Check a few out. They are pretty smart. It's like having a speech coach in your computer, asking you all the appropriate questions. Don't look too closely at the color scheme and overall design that the Wizard provides. All this can be changed easily. Just pay attention to the content—the sequence of slides and the text advice.

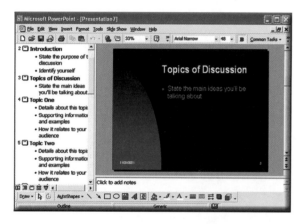

General Presentations

This category contains these outlines: Generic, Recommending a Strategy, Communicating Bad News, Training, Brainstorming Session, and Certificate. Here is the first slide from the Generic Presentation Outline. It contains nine slides with such "fill in the blanks" titles as Topics of Discussion, What This Means, and Next Steps. Of course, you can change the titles, captions, words, and pretty much everything else about it to make it personal, but Generic is a quick and dirty outline to use if you know exactly what you want to say.

Corporate Presentations

Under this category, you'll find six outlines: Business Plan, Financial Overview, Company Meeting, Employee Orientation, Group Home Page, Company Handbook. You're given direct advice on what to type in for your bullet points (such as "State specific measurable objectives" and "Outline your company's competitive advantage").

Project Presentations

Under the Projects button, you'll find Project Overview, Reporting Progress or Status, Project Post-mortem. Here is a sample slide from the Project Overview outline. It's an 11-slide primer for any kind of project. The slide on Technology and one of the two slides on Competitive Analysis may be overkill for some projects—but it's a simple thing to delete a slide that's not relevant to your presentation. And most of the slides—such as Procedures and Schedule—apply to every project.

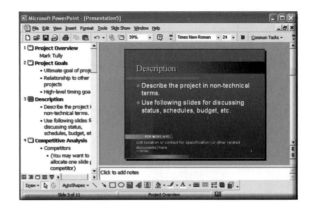

Sales/Marketing Presentations

Have to make a sales presentation? Click on any of these outlines. Here are the choices: Selling a product or service, Marketing plan, Product/services overview.

Carnegie Coach Presentations

This category is reserved for trickier presentations. It's named for the famed public speaking teacher Dale Carnegie. It has six outlines, namely: Selling Your Idea; Motivating a Team; Facilitating a Meeting; Presenting a Technical Report; Managing Organizational Change; Introducing and Thanking a Speaker. Carnegie Coach outlines have great pointers to help you create slides with language and examples that will resonate with your audience.

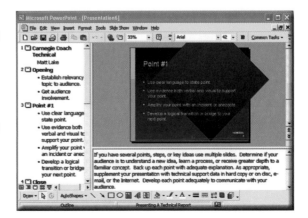

meet PowerPoint

$\mathbb{G}$reat, you've got PowerPoint up and running, and you've chosen the AutoContent Wizard Outline that works best for your presentation. And now you are staring at your very first PowerPoint slide. Since the technical terms can be a little daunting, here are some vocabulary tips. For starters, the entire window screen of presentation information is called a **slide**. What's tricky about slides is that you have to go back and forth between the two window **panes** (the outline pane where you can write notes that no one but you will see, and the inside pane, which is what the audience views.) More definitions to master:

A Outline pane

The text under the titles corresponds to what will appear in your slide. You can type in your text here.

B The slide preview

This is a smaller version of what your audience will see. In your presentation, it will fill the whole screen.

C Text formatting

This set of tools lets you change the font, size, and alignment of the text in your slides. The tools are pretty self-explanatory to anyone who's done word processing.

D Common tasks

Need to add a slide, apply a new design to your whole presentation, or add a new layout to your slide? Here's where you click to see the list of preset slide designs.

E Speaker notes

Here's where you make notes to yourself about each slide. Nobody but you will see these notes—they appear next to the slide when you print out your notes presentations.

F Drawing tools

Click here to add a double-headed arrow, create an organization chart, or add some clip art (see pages 170–171). This tool bar contains the basics.

G Change view tools

The screen layout in this picture isn't your only option. Click these buttons to see different layouts or to make your presentation fill the whole screen.

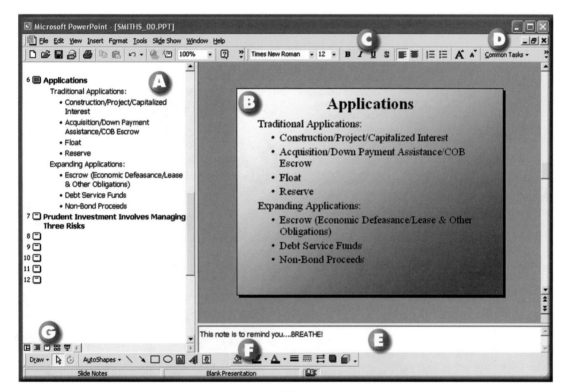

Here's a typical double-paned slide you will see when you create your presentation. The white pane is called the outline window that only you can see. The green pane is what your audience will see.

editing presentations

Okay, you've got the first slide up in the outline and you know what tools you can use. Now what? Now it's time to replace the PowerPoint words with your own. There are two ways to type in your own words.

1. You can click directly in the slide, highlight the words you want to replace, and then start typing.

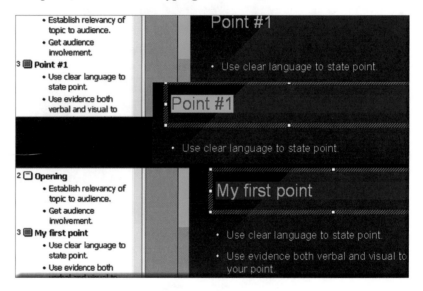

Highlight the words you want to replace (here it's Point #1). Then type "My first point," and it will replace it.

2. Or you can click in the little outline pane that runs down the left of the screen and type what you want and then cut and paste it as you would in a word processing program.

If you want to change the typeface (also known as **font**), highlight the text and then go up to Format and select Font. You can also make it bold or italic, give it a shadow, increase or decrease its size, or change its color.

When you are done with your presentation, save it as you would any other word processing file. Go up to File in the tool bar at the top of the screen and click on Save. PowerPoint will ask you to name the file and where you wish to store it.

STEP BY STEP: DELETING AND ADDING SLIDES

If the presentation outline you've chosen has more or fewer slides than you want, or if the facts suddenly change an hour before you're due to go on and you have to delete some slides or add new ones, don't worry. Here's how:

DELETING SLIDES

1. In the outline pane along the left side of the PowerPoint screen, move your mouse cursor over the little screen icon next to the slide's title.

2. The cursor will change shape from a pointer to a cross with arrows.

3. When you see the new cursor shape, click on the screen icon.

4. The slide's title and all the bullet points under it will be selected, and change from black text on a white background to white on black.

5. Press the Delete key and the slide will be deleted. All the subsequent slides will be renumbered.

ADDING NEW SLIDES

1. In the outline pane along the left side of the screen, click your mouse in the slide *before* the place you want to add a slide.

2. At the top right of the screen, locate the Common Tasks button. Click it and select New Slide.

3. You'll see a gallery of slide layouts. Click the one that matches the layout you want, such as the second in on the top row, which represents a standard title-and-bullet-points slide.

4. Click OK. Your new slide will appear.

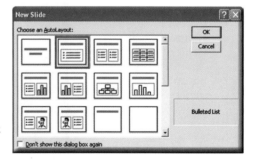

using design templates

Jazzing up your backgrounds

The outlines that come with AutoContent Wizard have standard (or default) background colors, fonts (typefaces), and background patterns. If you don't like the default, you can change it with the click of a mouse. How? There's a lot more to life than the color schemes and typestyles in PowerPoint's two dozen canned outlines. If you don't like the **font** (typestyles) or the slide **fill color** (background color) or the slide's **background textures** (patterns) or the **layout** (bullets, bar charts, etc.), you can change them. These cool features all fall under the **Design template** button. (A design template is computerspeak for the look or design of the screen.)

There are two ways to make changes to your presentation template. You can select the template first and then choose the AutoContent outline you want to use. (The Design Template option is the second option down, underneath AutoContent Wizard when you first launch PowerPoint.) Or you can apply a new design template to a presentation you've just created using the AutoContent Wizard Outline. Look under Format in the tool bar and click on Apply Design Template.

PowerPoint 2000 provides more than 40 different design templates to choose from. These templates mix different fonts, textures, and fill colors. Don't be put off by the strange words beginning with "Lorem Ipsum" in the preview! They are stand-ins so you can see the design with text.

STEP BY STEP: CHOOSING THE TEMPLATE FIRST

1. After you start up PowerPoint, select the Design Template button from the text box that appears. (Some older versions of PowerPoint call this button just Template.) Click OK. You'll have some design choices to make, so get ready to be the artiste.

2. First you need to select the overall Design Template. You'll see a list of template names for the background patterns, such as Artsy and Fireball. Click once on a few names and check out the preview picture until you see one you like. When you've made your selection, click OK.

3. PowerPoint will then start with a formatted slide with prompts such as Click to Add Title and Click to Add Text. This is where you type in your actual words.

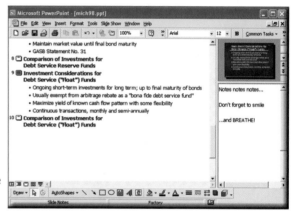

4. When you're done with your inputing of real live text, click on the Insert menu and select New Slide. You'll be presented with the New Slide dialogue box from step 3 again.

Continue this way—entering text, then selecting Insert and New Slide—until you complete all the slides in your presentation. Select File, then Save, to name and save your slides.

ADDING CLIP ART

You can also add clip art (techspeak for graphics) to your presentation to spice it up. PowerPoint comes with galleries of colorful illustrations to choose from—some whimsical, others simply decorative. To add PowerPoint clip art to your presentation, click on the right-hand column of the slide in which you want to add the art, click Insert, then Picture, and select Clip Art from the drop-down menu. Scroll through the gallery categories, such as Special Occasions, and click on an image you like. Then click Insert. A word of advice: Use clip art wisely; inappropriate art or too much art can make a presentation look tacky.

other PowerPoint features

Some really cool nuts and bolts you should know about

We've looked over some of the basic design features PowerPoint has to offer. But there are some special tools you really ought to know about for adding useful elements like bar charts (for figures), organization charts (for personnel), and some really fine background effects. Of course, any of these can be overused and detract from your message. But used well, they can keep your audience's attention.

Making Notes

Once you've created your slides, you can write out your speech text in PowerPoint directly below an image of the corresponding slide. Only you can see your talking points—the audience will simply view your slide. By printing out your presentation in the Notes Page view and using these pages as your manuscript, you'll have the security of having the right notes to the right slide right at your fingertips at all times. (It is set up to print out letter size.) This gives you more time to focus on your audience, rather than looking behind you to refer to the slide. Making notes is a breeze: Simply choose a slide you've already created, then select the View menu and then select Notes Page, and you will be presented with a box within which you can begin typing away.

Org Chart Editor

You can easily create org charts with Microsoft's Organization Chart feature. This is a separate program from PowerPoint, but PowerPoint can use it at will. Select Insert from the tool bar at the top, then select Object, and then scroll down the Object Type list to find Microsoft Organization Chart or MS Organization Chart 2.0 (depending on the version of Microsoft Office you're using). Select Okay. A window will pop up, and you can begin building your chart. When you're through, click the X to close, select Yes to save, and the Org Chart is automatically positioned in your PowerPoint presentation smack in the center of the slide where it looks best.

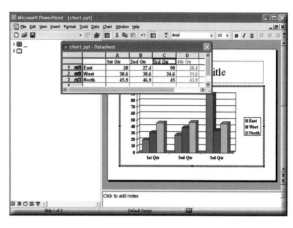

Chart Editor

If your presentation compares, say, sales figures by different divisions in different quarters,
the best way to show that information is with a
chart. PowerPoint uses Microsoft's Chart
Editor to create quick off-the-cuff bar charts
and other chart designs. Select the Insert menu
from the tool bar and click on Chart. A small spreadsheet with sample
data will appear, which is represented in your slide with a bar chart.
Change the data and the captions in the spreadsheet and the table will
change too. Once you're done, click the X in the data sheet title bar
and it will vanish, leaving your chart in the middle of the slide.

Fill Colors

If your slide's background seems dull or too dark, try creating a
gradual fill between background colors. This effect can look
really impressive, with a "sunrise" look as colors blend into
each other. Select Format/Background, then click on the down
arrow next to the color box underneath the main screen. Click
on the Fill Effects option. By clicking on the various options,
you can pick between any two colors and have the blends go
from more or less any angle, seeing previews as you go.

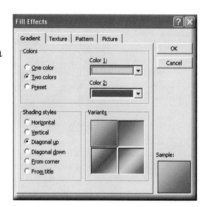

Background Textures

Another way to spruce up the background of your slides is to
add a texture to them. Select Format/Background, then click
on the down arrow next to the color box underneath the main
screen. Click on the Fill Effects option. Then click on the tab
labeled Texture and check out the gallery of texture effects.
The range on offer includes stone effects, wood, and various
fabrics. Some of these could be a little heavy for some presentations, but used well they can look great. You can change a
separate text box color. To do this, go up to Format, select
AutoShape (colors and lines). Just have the box you want to
change selected and click Change to Fill.

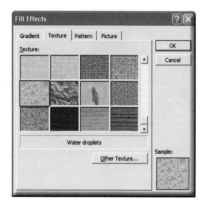

new views on your slides

Change your view for easier editing

For basic creative work and editing your slides, the **default** or standard PowerPoint screen we've been working with is just fine. But for fine-tuning your presentation, there are four completely different screen layouts, each of which works for different purposes. As you get more familiar with your slides, you may want to try a different perspective on your work.

These icons launch different views.

First, locate the View tool bar at the left, just underneath the outline and on top of the drawing tools in the Normal view. Then click on each of the options in turn.

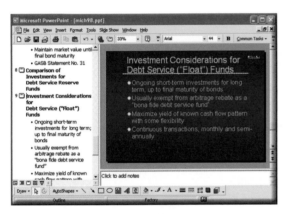

Normal View

There's a reason PowerPoint uses this view by default. It provides a nice large preview of the slide, but with plenty of room along the right for writing and editing the outline. But it's a little light on space for making notes (at the bottom, under the slide).

Outline View

Get distracted by graphics? You may prefer the outline view, which relegates the slide preview to a tiny little "thumbnail" in the top right, but gives you lots of space for developing your outline. There's also lots of room for jotting down speaker notes down the right. Tip: In this view, it's easy to rearrange the order of items in your outline by clicking once on their bullet points and dragging them up or down the list.

Slide View

You've done the creative outline and text editing work, and you're ready to proofread your work. Slide View is the one to do it in. You get to see and work on one slide at a time, but if you see an ugly line wrap or a glaring typo, you can easily edit text and graphics in this view. Want to spell check? Simply click in the slide you want and hit the F7 key.

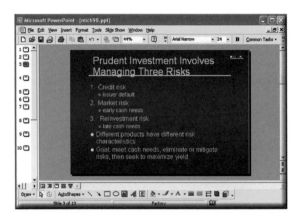

Slide Sorter View

Not to be confused with slide view, Slide Sorter View shows you a reduced-size storyboard of all your slides. This view is helpful to get an overview of the total look of your presentation, and it's the best view for changing the sequence of the slides—you just drag them with the mouse from one place to the other.

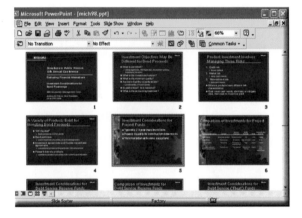

Slide Show View

Ready to take this show on the road? Then click on Slide Show View to see it as your audience will see it. Slide Show View removes all the editing tools, tool bars, and menus from your presentation, and fills your computer screen with each slide. Click on the mouse button (or spin the wheelie thing in the middle if you have a fancy mouse), and you'll move on to the next slide.

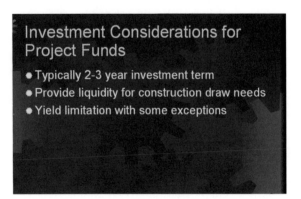

transitions

Moving from one slide to another

In regular slide shows, you moved from one slide to the other with the click of a button on the slide projector and a new 35mm slide popped up on the screen. The screen then went black for a moment, and a new picture appeared. Those were the good old boring days of presentations.

With PowerPoint, you can create very cool **transitions** (that's where you go from one slide to the next). You can have text flying in from any side of the screen, images appearing as though sheer curtains are swinging open to reveal them, or have an old slide dissolving to reveal a new slide underneath. If that seems too much, you can always fall back on the default or standard transition. That's where you click on a mouse button, the old slide disappears, and the new one appears in its place, just like a slide projector show, only a bit faster.

Jazzy transitions fall into several basic types. **Cuts** are the standard type—in which the old slide disappears and the new one appears. **Blinds** work like venetian blinds—strips of the new slide appear and cover up the old slide. **Box** and **checkerboard** transitions introduce the new image in square shapes (boxes are single large squares; checkerboards, lots of little ones). **Wipes**, **covers**, and **uncovers** slip new slides over the old ones. And **fades**, well . . . they fade images in and out. There is an animation preview, which lets you test a slide instead of viewing your whole show.

Note: If you're going to use fancy transitions, don't overuse them. If you're trying to get financing from investors, six different checkerboard transitions aren't going to impress; they're going to make you look frivolous.

STEP BY STEP: CREATING TRANSITION EFFECTS

1. In Slide View or Slide Sorter View, select the slide or slides you want to transition between.

2. In the Slide Show menu, click on Slide Transition.

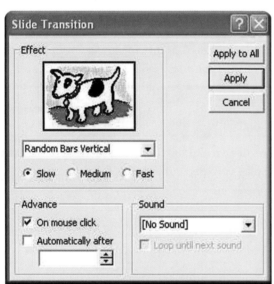

3. In the Effect box, click the transition you want—there are plenty to choose from, and you can see a preview of the effect in the little sample window.

4. You can select other options too, such as sound effects, but use these sparingly, since they tend to distract rather than support your message.

5. To apply the transition to the selected slide, click Apply, or click on Apply to All to make sure each slide gets the same transition (a good idea, since your audience won't spend all your presentation wondering what transition will come up next instead of listening to your words!).

Once you're done, be sure to check out how your transition looks in a real slide show. Click on the Slide Show menu, and select Animation Preview to get a preview. Bear in mind that transitions that look cute on a little preview thumbnail picture may not look so good when written large all over a screen.

build slides

Reinforce your key points visually

Remember that old lecturer at school who used overhead slides? Remember how he used a piece of paper to cover up the next point to prevent you from reading ahead as he made his point? Well, the visual effect was pretty dull, but there's no denying that if you want your audience to pay attention to your words, you should keep their eyes from wandering ahead.

Build slides do this trick in a visually appealing way. Let's say you want to justify your company's purchase of high-end server systems, and you have five bulleted points to support your argument. You display a slide of the first one:

Corporate Server Purchase

1. Increased productivity

You spend a minute or two elaborating on expected productivity increases, then display your second point as follows:

Corporate Server Purchase

1. Increased productivity

2. Industry leadership

Your first bulleted point remains, but recedes into the background as you discuss your second point. By the time you reach your fifth bulleted point, all your key points are displayed. The net effect of this technique is that each key point builds upon the next, providing visual reinforcement of your argument:

Corporate Server Purchase

1. Increased productivity

2. Industry leadership

3. Improved employee morale

4. Enhanced operations

5. Significant cost savings

So how do you make a build slide? Instructions appear on the following page.

ⓈTEP BY STEP: CREATING A BUILD SLIDE

1. In PowerPoint's New Slide screen, select the second slide template of a headline and bulleted text. Click OK.

2. Type in your headline and all five bullet points as you want them to appear in the final build slide.

3. Click on the Slide Show menu's Custom Animation option. Make sure only your bullet points are selected in the thumbnail view of your slide.

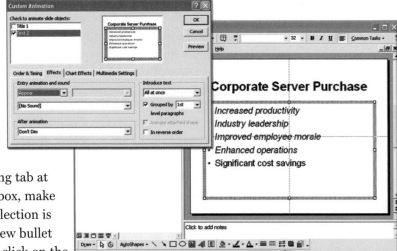

4. Under the Order & Timing tab at the bottom of the dialogue box, make sure the Start Animation selection is On. This means that your new bullet point will appear when you click on the mouse button during your presentation.

5. Click on the Effects tab, and under Entry Animation and Sound, make sure the animation list box shows Appear. (You could add a sound effect for each point, but this will probably just detract from your message in the actual presentation.)

6. Under After Animation, select a color for the previous bullet points (or select Don't Dim if you want them all to stay bold as you introduce new points).

7. Under Introduce Text, make sure All At Once appears in the list box instead of Letter by Letter or Word by Word.

8. Click on OK.

using blank presentations

Using your own creativity to create slides

See, you did it! Thanks to AutoContent Wizard you created your first presentation. Congratulations! If you are feeling bold and adventuresome, why not try creating your own PowerPoint presentation from scratch, especially if you aren't that keen on those pre-packaged outlines AutoContent Wizard provides.

When you first start PowerPoint, you can do just that by selecting the Blank Presentation option and clicking OK. Or if you've been working in PowerPoint for a while and want to start a new presentation with a clean slate, then you click on the File menu and select New. In the dialogue box that opens, click on Blank Presentation and you're ready to go.

You may choose to create plain slides or lace your presentation with all kinds of fun elements. It all depends on your message and your audience. PowerPoint gives you the option to do either. There are plenty of graphics and colors to work with. PowerPoint comes with quite a few preloaded graphic images that you can use to brighten up your presentation. See the next page for steps on how to create a nifty presentation from scratch.

CLIP ART ON THE WEB

Pictures often speak louder than words, so be sure to add one or two to your talk! There are a few Web sites that provide free graphics that you can download and add to your presentation. Once you've found the image you want, you need to click on it. A window will pop up asking you where you wish to save this art file. Save it to your hard drive (remember what file you store it in; feel free to rename it if you wish). To put it into a slide in your presentation, choose Insert from the tool bar, select Picture, then From File. From there you need to find the picture you saved on your hard drive.

Art Parts: **ronandjoe.com**

Artville: **artville.com**

Image Club Clip Art: **eyewire.com/products/clipart**

Ultimate Symbol: **ultimatesymbol.com**

Art Explosion: **novadevelopment.com**

STEP BY STEP: THE BLANK PRESENTATION

1. When you start PowerPoint, select Blank presentation and click OK.

2. In the New Slide (AutoLayout) screen, check out the thumbnail representations of layouts you might want. Click once on likely candidates and read the description underneath the OK button. You'll want to start out with the one in the top left corner, the title slide. When you've selected the slide layout, click on OK.

3. You'll see a blank slide with prompts "click to add title" and "click to add subtitle." Click on each in turn and enter your own text.

4. If you want to change the default typeface, select the text, then click on Format, then select Font. You can change the font, make it bold or italic, underline it, give it a shadow, increase or decrease its size, and even change its color.

5. To add a graphic (your PowerPoint software comes with some drawings called clip art), click on your slide in the right-hand column, click Insert, then Picture, and select Clip Art from the drop-down menu. Click on any of the Clip Art categories listed on the left to view the images. Select a category, such as People at Work, and click on an image you like. Then click Insert.

6. You'll see your slide complete with words and a picture. You can resize objects in your slide by running your cursor over one of the boxes until the cursor becomes an arrow, then holding down the mouse button and moving the mouse to decrease or increase the image size. You can move a text or picture box by placing the cursor over the outline and holding down the mouse.

That's one slide taken care of. Now add as many as you need for a full presentation, and apply a design template as the last step (see page 160 for details).

printing and presenting

No job's ever quite done without the paperwork

No matter how impressive your presentation, nobody's going to remember all of it without a few memory joggers—and that even includes you! So when you're done with your PowerPoint presentation, the next step is to see what leave-behinds and speaker's notes the program lets you create.

The first rule of printing from PowerPoint is to ignore the little Print icon in the tool bar. That just prints out your entire presentation, one slide per page, and there are much better options available. So what does PowerPoint let you print out? Here's a breakdown.

Slides The default setting prints one page per slide and ignores any build effects you may have in place.

Slides with builds If you have a build in place and want your handouts to reflect this, a second print option prints all the slides, one per page, and puts each bulleted item you add in your build on its own page. This will more accurately reflect the course of your presentation if you want people to follow along.

Handouts If you want to cut down on rustling during your presentations or just save paper, handouts are the way to go. This print setting prints two, three, or six slides per page in thumbnail format.

Notes Pages Those speaker notes you so scrupulously wrote out can be printed out separately too, so you can practice your presentation before you go on without having to have a computer on. Notes pages can also be handed out as a reference for the audience.

Outline View Prints an outline just as it appears along the right side of your screen.

STEP BY STEP: PRINTING BASICS

1. In PowerPoint, bring up the Print dialogue box (click on the File menu's Print option, or hold down the Ctrl key and press P).

2. At the bottom of the Print dialogue box, you'll see all your options in a list box labeled Print What.

3. To print slides one per page, make sure Slides appears in the Print What list box. If you have build effects in your presentation and want them reflected in your handouts, click to place a checkmark in the box labeled Include Animations. The slides will print in color unless you click a checkmark in either the Grayscale or Pure Black and White box.

4. To print handouts, select Handouts in the Print What list, and then select the number of slides per page and other features in the Handouts area.

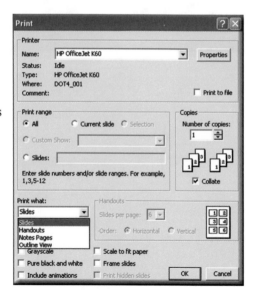

5. The other print options, Notes Pages and Outline View, are simple selections in the Print What list box.

6. When you've made your selection, click the OK button and the presentation will print out.

tips for using slides

Slides can bring impact to your words

Complementing your talk with slides can increase your audience's understanding and recall of your message. These tips will help you use slides to your greatest advantage.

Choosing your colors

■ Select two or three background colors (see page 176) and use them consistently. More colors will distract.

■ Use dark colors for background and light colors for text.

■ Be aware that some audience members may be "color-blind." Avoid color combinations such as red and green, brown and green, blue and black.

■ Use red carefully—it is a powerful color, but can also signify financial loss.

Laying out the text

■ Use a large, easily read typeface, preferably sans serif like Universal or Arial (see page 189). Use boldface sparingly.

■ Keep text to a minimum. Five to seven words per line, five to seven lines per slide.

■ Begin each line with a verb, adjective, or noun. Be consistent!

■ Leave a border of blank space around the perimeter of each slide. Text that goes right to the edge can get cut off when projected.

Selecting graphics

■ Use solid colors to fill bar charts and other graphics rather than patterns such as cross hatching and dots. To do this, click on Format in the tool bar and then click on Color and Lines. Patterns don't project well.

■ Vary the graphics, alternately using pie charts, bar charts, and line graphs.

■ Size scanned images (such as photography) appropriately. Stretching or shrinking a scanned image can affect its resolution quality.

Presenting your slides

■ Introduce yourself and your message first, before projecting anything other than a title or logo slide.

■ Don't just read what's on your slides; blend the bullets naturally into your speech.

■ Introduce each slide with an overview comment, then project the slide.

Always bring a spare disk of your presentation. You never know when you might need it.

FIRST PERSON — DISASTER STORY

Projector preparation

It was my first PowerPoint presentation at my new client's office. I had worked on the presentation for days, and rehearsed my talk. I was raring to go. I had even brought a backup disk just in case of a problem. The problem turned out to be far more basic: The connecting cables between my laptop and their projector were not compatible. I wish I had called ahead to check that out. Worst case scenario: Always bring a printout of your presentation. I had to wing the whole thing from memory.

Susan S., Phoenix, Arizona

now what do I do?

Answers to common questions

Is it possible to merge two presentations into one?

Absolutely. Begin with the first presentation, and select Insert/Slides from File command. Using the Slide Sorter View, you can reorganize and re-sequence your slides. You can copy slides from one presentation to another by going to Slide Sorter View, highlighting the slide you want to copy, selecting Copy, opening the other presentation, and selecting Paste.

How can I change the default colors?

PowerPoint templates come with a number of alternate color schemes. Go to the tool bar at the top, select Format, then select Color Scheme, then Standard to choose a different palette of colors.

How can I ensure that the text in my slides will be visible to everyone?

Experts say the "8H" rule is the best way to make sure that even the folks in the back row can read the text on your slides. This rule states that the maximum viewing distance (from the back of the auditorium to the front) should not be more than eight times the height of the projection screen. If that condition is met, as long as your text is at least 1/50th the height of the screen, then it should be legible from the back of the room.

A slide projected on a computer screen should contain text no smaller than 11 pt. type. For slides projected on a large screen, 22 pt. type should work best.

How do I change the background color of my slides?

Easily. Select Format/Background, then click on the down arrow next to the color box underneath the main screen. Scroll to find the background color or pattern you'd like. Click Apply. There are also some cool background effects described on page 163, which you can get at when you click on the Fill Effects option.

Can I spell check a PowerPoint slide?

Yes. Just select the slide you want to check, then press F7.

How do I align the text in a PowerPoint presentation?

Piece of cake. Highlight the text in the slide you want to align differently. From the Format menu, select Alignment, then choose from Left, Right, Center, or Justify (for text that lines up straight down the left and right).

Now where do I go?!

CONTACTS	PUBLICATIONS
www.microsoft.com/office/powerpoint Microsoft PowerPoint site	**Using Microsoft PowerPoint 2000 Special Edition** by Patrice-Anne Rutledge
desktoppub.about.com/cs/powerpoint/ About PowerPoint (general tips)	**PowerPoint 2000 For Windows For Dummies** by Doug Lowe
desktoppub.about.com/cs/powerpointadv/ About PowerPoint (advanced tips)	**PowerPoint 2000/98 for Windows and Macintosh: Visual QuickStart Guide** by Rebecca Bridges Altman

CHAPTER 10

From start to finish

You get "the call"
Visualize success like an athlete **180**

Two weeks to go
Create a schedule and checklists **182**

Ten days to go
Research your topic **184**

One week to go
Writing out your presentation **186**

Five days to go
Smart visual aids **188**

One day to go 190

The morning of your talk 191

Ten minutes to go 192

You're on! 193

Almost over! 194

Closing statement 195

Now what do I do?
Answers to common questions **196**

Ready, set, go. You're on. Stride across the stage with confidence and enthusiasm.

you get "the call"

Like an athlete, visualize your success before you step up to the plate

Being asked to speak to a group is like being called up from the minors and sent to the big leagues. It's an opportunity to stand apart from the rest, literally and figuratively. It's a chance to demonstrate your talent, uniqueness, and value to the organization. When you step up to the podium, dust it off like you own it and seize the opportunity to show everyone what you've worked so hard to attain.

Great baseball players bring more than skill to the game—they bring heart. With every swing, they demonstrate their passion, personality, and confidence. They practice hard to keep their edge.

And because they work so hard at their game, every time they connect with the ball, it's a pure thrill. You too will feel that thrill. After all the preparation and practice you put into your talk, you and your message will connect with your audience to score big. And just as ballplayers are cheered on by their fans, you too will reap sincere appreciation from your audience after you deliver a well-crafted and ably delivered talk.

The following pages offer tips that consolidate much of the available wisdom from the pros and from the preceding pages. Use these tips well, and they won't ever fail you.

KEEPING COOL WHEN YOU FIRST LEARN
YOU WILL GIVE A TALK

■ Turn your negative thoughts into positive ones. Examples: "I know this topic inside and out," "It's a great career move," and "I am uniquely qualified to do this."

■ End a spiral into negativity by yelling to yourself, "STOP!!!" This will jolt you back to reality so you can work on thinking positively.

■ Remind yourself that there are few better ways to prove your leadership ability than by addressing an audience.

■ Know that your credibility among your peers and superiors is about to skyrocket.

■ Dive into this opportunity with abandon and an open mind.

■ Channel your nervousness into quiet excitement.

■ Tell colleagues and friends that you'll be speaking. You'll be building support before you even begin writing your presentation.

■ Visualize yourself standing confidently at the podium, communicating your expertise as well as your topic.

■ Remember that your attitude drives your nerves. Be open, receptive, and enthusiastic about this remarkable opportunity, and your nerves will settle.

■ Act "as if." Even if, inwardly, you dread this assignment, act as if you welcome it. Your actions will catch up with your thoughts.

two weeks to go

Put yourself on a schedule while you chart the course of your talk

One of the keys to being a confident speaker is being prepared. No matter how well you know your subject, presenting it cohesively and convincingly takes thought and preparation.

Ideally, you'll have a few weeks to put your presentation together. Working backward from the day you're scheduled to present your topic, you can determine how much time you have to prepare for it. And every minute will count, since you'll be filling that time with organizing, researching, writing, rehearsing, and fine-tuning your talk.

Even before you begin to organize your material, you should prepare a checklist to get answers to questions that will help you determine the mission of your talk, the tone you will take, and what approach will help you get the outcome you desire. Don't overlook the obvious questions, either—sometimes they are the most important. Questions such as "Who is in the audience?" and "Why are they there?" are critical, because you won't achieve your goals if you don't consider the needs of your audience.

SAMPLE TALK PREPARATION TIME LINE

Presentation date: _____

Number of days until talk: _____

Finalize topic by: _____

Finalize research by: _____

Prepare outline by: _____

Write presentation by: _____

Prepare slides and handouts by: _____

Proofread slides/charts/handouts by: _____

PREPARE A CHECKLIST OF QUESTIONS

Audience

■ Who will attend my talk?

■ Is their attendance mandatory, or are they attending because they are interested in my topic?

■ Will they be accepting of or hostile toward my point of view?

■ How much do they already know about my topic?

Room Setup

■ How large is the room? (How many people are expected to attend?)

■ How will the chairs be set up?

■ Will I be able to project slides or use any type of audiovisuals?

■ Phone at center stage?

Talk Organization

■ What do I want to accomplish with my talk?

■ What is the one thing I want each audience member to remember?

■ How should I present my topic? Am I trying to inform, persuade, or motivate?

Talk Logistics

■ Who is sponsoring the meeting at which I will speak?

■ Is there a theme for the seminar?

■ Who else is speaking?

■ How long do I have to speak?

■ Is there time for a Q&A?

■ Can I distribute handouts?

ten days to go

Pump up your presentation with fascinating facts

Great material is memorable, new, and relevant. Use these tips to find the best information for your presentation.

If you are addressing a group of colleagues from your company, the first place to search is internal corporate sources such as press releases, marketing materials, advertising, executive speeches, and annual reports. You'd be amazed at what treasures your company already has on hand.

When you have mined your corporate resources, look to external sources for information on current events that will make your presentation timely. Use sources like print and TV news coverage, analysts' reviews of business trends, and trade publications.

It's also good to round out your presentation with surprising facts. What else happened in history on the day you are to speak? Was a famous battle waged that day, or does a patron saint have a feast day in common with your speaking engagement? (Imagine speaking on December 20, the feast day for St. Dominic, patron saint of prisoners and captives. You could tell your audience that in recognition of the day, you promise not to hold them captive for more than 30 minutes.) Where do you get this kind of information? If you can't find it yourself on the Internet, make friends with your local librarian. Typically fonts of information, reference librarians are skilled at using enormously helpful (though not particularly user-friendly) online databases such as Lexis/Nexis.

GREAT RESEARCH WEB SITES

Get crazy on the Internet. Use a variety of search engines to uncover interesting facts that amplify and illuminate your subject. Search for great quotations that capture your central ideas. If nothing else, find out what's been said before on your topic and build on it with a unique perspective.

Dogpile.com (search engine)

Google.com (search engine)

Altavista.com (search engine)

Webcrawler.com (search engine)

Idea-bank.com (quotations, speech resources)

Bartleby.com (quotations, references)

Harpers.org (*Harper's* magazine)

rd.com (*Reader's Digest* magazine)

Nationalgeographic.com (*National Geographic* magazine)

Npr.org (National Public Radio)

Demographics.com (*American Demographics* magazine)

Nytimes.com (*The New York Times*)

Newsdirectory.com (links to online international newspapers)

Findarticles.com (links to articles from over 300 magazines)

Loc.gov (Library of Congress)

Gallup.com (Gallup research organization)

Salon.com (online magazine, intriguing editorial content)

one week to go

Organize and write for maximum effect

You've thought through what you want to say and have pulled together and organized your research and key points into an outline. Now what? Now it's time to write your presentation. In a nutshell, here's how it should flow:

For starters, grab them with a strong opening (for more info, see page 48). Your opening statement should make your audience sit up and listen. Spark their interest with your humor, a benefit you can provide them, or a question they will want answered.

Transition to the purpose of your talk (see page 22). Describe what you will cover and what you expect to accomplish.

Move into the body with its key points (see page 50). Present your key points in an order best suited to your topic, i.e., chronologically, geographically, problem/solution, or by category.

Briefly summarize your talk. This is called the wrap-up (see page 54). You'll be "telling 'em what you told 'em," but the repetition can drive the message home. After you summarize, transition to a Q&A period if it's appropriate for your talk (see page 56).

Leave them with a knockout closing statement that makes it clear what you want them to do, know, expect, or remember as a result of your talk (see page 56).

All done? Great! Now clear your throat and try speaking your words out loud, alone. When you stumble over a word or phrase that doesn't sound right, rewrite it. Avoid big or unfamiliar words. In the heat of a presentation, you can trip over them. Once you like the sound of your speech, practice, practice, practice.

DRAFTING YOUR SCRIPT

■ Always write for the ear, not the eye. That means write the way you speak!

■ Don't be afraid of beginning sentences with "And . . ." or "But . . ." They can be effective devices to link thoughts and ideas.

■ Keep your writing clear. Don't cloud your message with jargon, corporatespeak, or clichés.

■ Write in the active, not passive voice. Example: "Teamwork solves problems" sounds stronger than "When teamwork is used, the problems are solved."

■ Write out numbers, use phonetic spellings, or put dashes in acronyms to help you pronounce your words correctly. Examples: write "one million dollars" (instead of $1,000,000); "Ronald RAY-gen" (not REEgan); V-A-T (not VAT).

■ Make it personal with your own anecdotes, observations, ideas.

■ Use quotes, metaphor, humor, analogy, and/or simile to drive your point home.

■ Express your points using a positive, not negative, viewpoint. Studies show that concepts expressed in the negative are more difficult to grasp.

five days to go

Using design and words for impact

Great! Your speech is written and you like the way it sounds. Now it's time to consider using visual aids to give it just the impact it needs. There are lots of A/V devices to choose from (see page 128), but if you want your presentation to be effective, you should choose and use your A/V tools judiciously. The design of 35mm or PowerPoint slides and handouts is particularly important. Here are some tips to guide you:

For Slides

Keep your text to a minimum. Your slides should tell their story at a glance, with just a few spare bullets per slide. Otherwise your text becomes a distraction and you risk losing your audience's focus on you. Remember, your slides should support what you say, not substitute for it. They should directly follow the outline of your remarks.

Your language should be consistent from slide to slide, that is, begin each bullet point with a verb or noun, and stick to that style throughout your presentation. Don't forget to spell check AND proofread your work. Typos and misspellings look even worse when magnified on a screen.

Designing your slides takes some restraint, since the impulse is to experiment with all the cool PowerPoint options once you know how to use them. When choosing colors, select two or three and use them consistently. Dark colors work best for background, light for text. Red is very difficult to read on a dark background, and it can have negative connotations (i.e., warning, deficit), so use red judiciously. Some audience members may be color-blind, so try to avoid combinations such as red and green, brown and green, and blue and black.

Sans serif typefaces, such as Arial and Universal, have no curly flourishes. They are highly legible and work best for text slides. Never use ALL UPPERCASE IN YOUR BULLETS because it reads like you are yelling at your audience. If that's not your intention, stay away from all uppercase.

When you use graphics such as pie charts, bar charts, and line graphs, vary them to keep your audience's attention. Use solid colors to fill bar charts rather than patterns such as cross-hatching or dots. Patterns don't project as well as solids. And when you insert a photo or clip art into your slides, size them carefully! Stretching or shrinking a scanned image can cause distortion and can affect its resolution quality.

FOR HANDOUTS

Your handouts should be considered a stand-alone presentation. Imagine that the person who receives them was not able to attend your talk—would he or she understand your key points just by reading a hard copy of your slides? When you prepare your handouts, include sub-bullets under your key points to expand on and clarify them. Make sure you include a title page with your name, date of the presentation, and company affiliation. It's also a good idea to put your contact information into a header or footer on each page of your handout.

one day to go

Rehearse till it just comes naturally

With one day to go before you address your audience, you'll want to use the time to rehearse. If possible, rehearse in the room in which you'll actually be presenting. You'll feel more familiar with the room and become comfortable with the audiovisual equipment.

Ask a few friends to listen to you rehearse. One friend should have an intimate knowledge of your subject; the other should be only peripherally knowledgeable about it. Have them sit at opposite ends of the room to ensure that you can be heard. One person should time you to make sure you keep within the time allotted for your talk. Practice making eye contact with your guests, and be sure to rehearse with your audiovisual requirements, such as slides or video. When you've concluded your rehearsal, ask each individual for honest feedback about your presentation. Which parts weren't clear? Was the flow right? Listen to their comments and fine-tune your presentation accordingly.

the morning of your talk

Presenting the very best you

Your appearance, demeanor, and body language should communicate the professionalism and credibility you're trying to get across in your speech. These tips will help you make sure they do.

Find out what the dress code is for the day and dress one level better. Shoes should be shined and the bottoms scuffed so you don't slide across the stage. Wear a blouse with a collar or a sports jacket with a lapel for a clip-on microphone.

Choose any jewelry carefully. Men's sport rings or college rings can be large and heavy, and may clank on the podium when you put your hand down. Women should stay away from very sparkly earrings or necklaces, as they reflect light and can distract your audience. Necklaces and bracelets shouldn't dangle near the microphone.

Men should keep double-breasted suit jackets buttoned. Single-breasted jackets can be worn unbuttoned. And never wear short socks onstage! Knee-length socks are a must. Empty your pockets of change before you speak to resist the urge to jingle. Ties can be colorful but not distracting. When choosing the clothes in which you'll present, ask yourself, would I listen to a speaker if he were dressed like this?

Women have more options when it comes to clothing, and with more options comes more opportunities to make a mistake. Avoid clothes with large patterns and optical designs. Leave that fussy scarf and stiletto heels at home. Choose a more conservative outfit so the focus is on you and not on your clothes.

Avoid caffeine and dairy products that morning. You'll be charged up naturally anyway! Before the meeting begins, do a once-over in the rest-room mirror. Make sure hair and clothing are in place, your name badge is on straight, and there are no surprises between your teeth. In fact, bring a toothbrush, toothpaste, and mouthwash to use just before the meeting starts. Wait! Before you turn away from the mirror, smile at yourself confidently because you look terrific, you are ready, and you will do a great job!

ten minutes to go

Control your fear from the get-go

Fear is a natural and common reaction to public speaking. That's why you need to turn your negative thoughts into positive ones. When you feel the panic start to rise, stop the spiral into negativity by saying to yourself: "I know this topic inside and out," or "It's a great career move," or "I am uniquely qualified to do this." Another good tactic is to remind yourself that there are few better ways to prove your leadership ability than by addressing an audience.

Visualize yourself standing confidently at the podium, communicating your expertise as well as your topic. Then radiate that confidence! Warmly greet the people arriving to hear you talk. This way, when you face them from the podium, they are no longer a threatening sea of faces, but people you've already met that came by to learn something from you. Believe it or not, pretending that you

are confident can do an end run around your fears. This is because our actions are based on our feelings and thoughts. Try to psych yourself into not feeling afraid or nervous and you won't be.

If all else fails, however, and you find yourself anxiously counting down the minutes and seconds until your presentation, STOP! Instead, breathe rhythmically and deeply to relax yourself. Slow down. A final note: Never use alcohol or drugs to calm down. You want to be sharp and quick, not hazy and slow.

you're on!

You can do it!

Ready, set, go, you're on! Stride across the stage with confidence and enthusiasm, shoulders back, head up. Take your place at the podium, then pause for a few seconds to organize your papers and get set for your talk. Use that pause to build anticipation in the audience. Now take a few steps back from the podium so that you don't have to bend your face down to read your lines. Breathe from the belly to relax your diaphragm and massage your lungs. The more air you deliver to your lungs, the deeper and richer your voice will be.

As you begin speaking, use your voice as a resource. Vary the pitch, tone, inflection, and speed of your delivery. Speak more slowly when presenting key points, and build pauses into your talk. They get attention and also allow your audience to digest what you've just said.

Be microphone-savvy. Don't turn away from it and talk (it may sound obvious, but how often have you seen it happen?) If your hands are trembling, don't hold your speech or a microphone in your hands. Use the table or podium for your script and a stand for the microphone.

As you talk, use movements and facial expressions you'd normally use in conversation. But like a performer, make these movements broader to suit the size of your audience. Keep eye contact. Vary the direction in which you look, and vary your hand gestures.

Keep your elbows bent and arms apart, resting on the podium—definitely don't let them droop lamely by your sides. And avoid defensive postures, such as arms folded across your chest and legs crossed.

Try not to point at anyone in the audience, even when calling on people during a Q&A. It's never perceived as a friendly or elegant gesture.

Finally, act as if you enjoy being there. Audiences love confident and enthusiastic speakers, and the support and anticipation from your listeners will help you relax.

almost over!

Sending them off in style

You're almost done! A lot of speakers are so relieved at this point that they lose their focus and give short shrift to the Q&A period and closing statement. Don't fall into the same trap. The Q&A is vital to ensuring that your audience really understood you, and the closing statement is your last chance to fulfill the mission of your talk. These tips will help you close your session with the impact you want.

Handling Q&A's

Let your audience know at the outset if you'll be taking questions at the end of your presentation. When you are done with your presentation, say that you will now take questions. If you want to control the amount of time dedicated to the Q&A, let them know how much time will be devoted to it.

Let the questioner finish his or her question before beginning your response. Repeat the question if you are addressing a large group. Maintain eye contact with the questioner while the question is being asked, but resume eye contact with your audience while you give your answer.

If you don't know the answer, don't apologize. Tell the questioner that you will get back to him or her after the talk, and then do it. If your questioner is aggressive, be polite but firm. Don't become aggressive in turn. Offer to discuss the issue after the talk, and point out that others should be given a chance to pose their questions.

When it's time to end the Q&A session, let your audience know when you will take one final question.

closing statement

Send them off with a powerful message

Don't end your presentation with your last answer to a question. Get your audience's attention back on your presentation by ending with a powerful closing statement. Here are some tips:

If your goal is to inspire your audience to action or to change their thinking, appeal to emotion. Use language that paints a picture in their minds, or try a thought-provoking quote, statistic, or fact to conclude your talk.

This is the last opportunity you have to make an impression on your audience, so don't ruin it by racing through your closing statement. For example, don't gather up your pens, notes, etc. while you are making your closing statement. You and your audience should be totally focused on your final words.

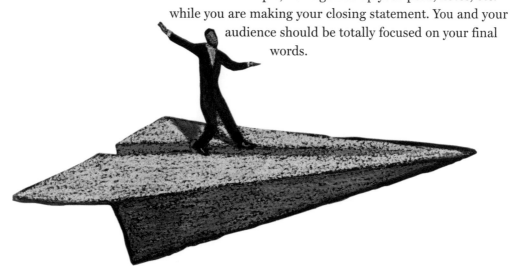

now what do I do?

Answers to common questions

Should I type or handwrite my presentation?

Typing is best because it's easier to read. Use large type—12 pt. is good, 14 pt. is even better—and boldface it. Type in upper- and lowercase. Never read from a script in all uppercase—it's difficult to read and it plays havoc with acronyms. Double-space between lines of text, and keep your margins wide. Use a wide left margin to pencil in A/V cues or other notes to yourself. Mark your script with cues to slow down, emphasize certain words, or pause. Use colored pens and highlighters. End each page with a full sentence, and don't split paragraphs at the bottom of a page.

I am representing my company at a large corporate dinner. I am so nervous about speaking that I don't think I can eat a bite. What should I do?

Try to settle your nerves by visualizing your success. Don't worry about eating—you can always have someone save you a plate of food for after your presentation. Whatever you do, don't drink alcohol to assuage your fears. You want to harness that nervous energy and use it to energize your presentation. But since the first few minutes of speaking are usually the most unnerving, memorize your opening remarks. This way, you'll breeze right through the dreaded first few minutes, and you just may surprise yourself and find out that once you're up there, you enjoy the experience after all.

I have practiced my presentation until I am blue in the face, but I am still nervous. What can I do to calm down once I'm at the podium?

Look at your watch, and remind yourself that in 30 minutes, no matter what happens, your presentation will be over and you can get on with your life! Another trick is to wear a rubber band around your wrist and snap it whenever you feel yourself sinking into fear. It literally helps you "snap out of it." Perhaps your child gave you a lucky pebble or other object to help get you through your talk. Pat your suit pocket to feel it, or if it's tiny, place it on the podium where no one else can see it. It will be a constant reminder of something familiar and safe. There's comfort in the familiar!

My talk is being videoconferenced to our Hong Kong office. Any suggestions for running a smooth meeting?

Electronic meetings present some unique problems. Here are some pointers: Send the meeting agenda, handouts, and speaker bios to the remote office ahead of time so they can review them before you meet. Assume that you are always visible on camera, so act accordingly. Ask for feedback often—you want to be sure that the remote office can hear and understand you. Women should stay away from flame-red lipsticks or other bright shades, as they tend to bleed on camera. Men and women should consider powdering their faces to prevent glare from shiny skin. Geometric or too-tight pinstripe patterns can cause optical illusions on the receiving side, so stay away from them.

After my presentation, I have to be interviewed by a local TV network. Is there anything I should do to prepare for that?

Remember what the main purpose of your talk is, and choose two or three key points to support it. No matter what question you are asked, your answer should include only your key points. It can feel awkward at first, but this way you can be sure that if you make the nightly news, the message that you want told will be told. (If you choose to answer a question that is not related to your key point, then just know that they will edit your answer and you won't know what will be used.) Above all, be polite and professional. Let the interviewer finish his or her question before you answer.

OW WHERE DO I GO?!

PUBLICATIONS

Smart Speaking
by Laurie Schloff
and Marcia Yudkin

glossary

Acronym A word formed from the initial letters of a name, such as WAC for Women's Army Corps.

Active voice In sentences written in the active voice, the subject performs the action expressed in the verb. Use the active voice to get your message across. Example: "Our director slashed the budget." (See passive voice.)

Alliteration The repetition of the same letters or sounds at the beginning of a series of words, as in "puffy plumes of powder."

Analogy A comparison between two otherwise dissimilar things. For example, "Running a business is in many ways like conducting an orchestra. You have one leader and a group of people, and each person has individual responsibilities, but everyone must work together as one for the result to be successful."

Anecdote A short account of an interesting or humorous incident.

Attribution The act of crediting a particular person as the writer of a quote or passage.

Blocking To indicate broadly (i.e., "block out") your onstage movements in relation to the podium or other large props on stage.

Body language Messages conveyed nonverbally through physical gestures and postures.

Breakout sessions Small-group meetings that convene concurrently during a conference, typically to study one aspect of the conference theme.

Downstage The front of the stage, closest to the audience.

Font A complete set of type of one size and face. For example, Courier is a font.

Impromptu speech Speaking with little preparation and no notes.

Informative speech A speech that is designed to impart knowledge or clarify a concept.

Jargon The specialized or technical language of a trade, profession, or similar group.

Keynote The featured speech at a program or conference. The featured speaker is also known as the keynoter.

Lavaliere A wireless microphone, typically worn clipped to a speaker's lapel.

Lectern A reading stand with a slanted top, often placed upon a table, from which to read a speech.

Metaphor A figure of speech in which a word or phrase that ordinarily designates one thing is used to designate another, as in "an ocean of love," and "drowning in fear."

Moderator One who presides over a meeting, forum, or debate.

Modulation A change in stress, pitch, loudness, or tone of the voice; an inflection of the voice.

Motivational speech A speech that is intended to inspire, motivate, or build confidence among audience members.

Overhead projector A projector with a light source in the base of the machine. Light is projected up through a lens in the projector's head and then onto a screen.

Oxymoron A phrase composed of incongruous or contradictory terms, such as a deafening silence and a mournful optimist.

Panel A group of experts brought together to share the stage while presenting a topic from their point of view.

Parody A literary or artistic work that imitates the characteristic style of an author or a work for comic effect.

Passive voice In sentences written in the passive voice, the subject receives the action expressed in the verb. Passive writing is less effective at communicating your message. Example: "The budget was cut by our director." (See active voice.)

Persuasive speech A speech that is designed to move an audience to take an action or change a belief.

Pitch The distinctive quality of the sound of one's voice. Depending on the relative position of this sound (within a range of sounds), a person could have a high-pitched voice or a low-pitched voice.

Podium An elevated platform from which to read a speech.

Range The gamut of tones that a voice is capable of producing.

Search engine A Web site whose primary function is to provide a search engine for gathering information available on the Internet.

Seminar Typically a daylong program with presentations, breakout sessions, and/or panel discussions.

Simile Two essentially unlike things are compared, often in a phrase introduced by like or as. Example: "My love is like a red, red rose."

Speakers bureau An agency that represents and markets professional speakers to corporations and trade associations.

Stage left The area to the left of center stage when facing the audience.

Stage right The area to the right of center stage when facing the audience.

Teleprompter A machine that displays to a speaker an enlarged line-by-line reproduction of a script, unseen by the audience.

Template A document or file having a preset format, used as a starting point for a particular application so that the format does not have to be re-created each time it is used. Example: a loan amortization template for a spreadsheet program.

Transition Words, phrases, or sentences that provide smooth flow from one idea or topic to another in a speech.

Transparencies The transparent film used with overhead projectors. Also called foils, overheads, or acetates.

Upstage The rear, or back, of the stage (or to grab the spotlight away from someone else!).

URL An Internet address (for example, http://www.idea-bank.com), usually consisting of the access protocol (http) and the domain name (www.idea-bank.com).

index

A

accents, regional, 76
acronyms, 76
active voice, 52, 187
Adobe Photoshop, 147
adrenaline, 10
agendas, place on, 17
Allen, Steve, 29
Altman, Rebecca Bridges, 177
American Demographics magazine, 33
analogies, 34, 37, 46
anecdotes, 24–25, 37, 46. *See also* humor
    opening with, 49
    sources for, 32–33
anxiety. *See* fear
apologies, 55
appearance, 78–91
    dress, 17, 191
    dress and, 88–89
    for men, 91
    physical presence in, 86–87
    videoconferences and, 197
    for women, 90
articulation, 70, 73
attitude, 181
    audience, 112–125
    attention span of, 23
    body language of, 113, 122–123
    chatting with, 81
    comfort of, 101, 107, 120–121
    engaging, 14–15
    expectations of, 116–117
    expressing gratitude to, 34, 81
    getting information about, 124
    hecklers, 125
    hostile, 124
    humor and, 124
    inspiring, 54
    knowing who they are, 16, 114–115
    large, 115, 124
    maintaining interest of, 24–25
    Q&A sessions, 55
    regaining attention of, 123
    test, 118–119
    types of speeches and, 94–95, 99
    young, 110

B

Bachner, Jane, 77
background colors, 174–175, 176
background textures, 160, 163
being yourself, 48
Bell, Alexander Graham, 28
Bienvenu, Sherron, 77
blinds, 166
body language, 66, 82–83, 193
    audience, 113, 122–123
body of presentations, 186
    outlining, 42
    writing, 50–51
books
    Articulate Executive, 77
    Bartlett's Familiar Quotations, 32
    *Complete Idiot's Guide to Public
        Speaking*, 19
    Encyclopedia Britannica, 33
    Great Presentation Skills, 59, 91, 197
    *How to Develop Self-Confidence and
        Influence People by Public
        Speaking*, 19
    How to Speak Like a Pro, 19
    *How to Write and Deliver an Effective
        Speech*, 77
    Inspire Any Audience, 19
    *Marketing and Promoting Your Own
        Seminars and Workshops*, 111
    *100 Best Companies to Work for in
        America*, 25
    *PowerPoint 2000 For Windows and
        Macintosh: Visual QuickStart
        Guide*, 177

PowerPoint 2000 For Windows For Dummies, 177
Presentation Skills Workshop, 77
Seminars: The Emotional Dynamic, 111
Seminar Selling: The Ultimate Resource Guide to Marketing Financial Services, 111
7 Steps to Fearless Speaking, 19
Speaking Up, 77
Speak Smart, 59, 91, 197
Using Microsoft PowerPoint 2000, 177
Who Moved My Cheese?, 136
box transitions, 166
brands, value of, 25
breathing, 13, 192
   correct method for, 68–69
Brown, Jay, 24
build slides, 168–169
Bush, George H.W., 28
business casual attire, 89
business dress attire, 89

C

caffeine, 191
calls for action, 54
calm, how to maintain, 12–13.
     See also fear
Carnegie, Dale, 19, 155
casual attire, 89
categorical organization, 50
causal order, 40
   for informational talks, 97
charts, 146, 189
   flip, 140–141, 145
   organization, 162
   PowerPoint, 151, 162–163
checkerboard transitions, 166
Chesterton, Gilbert Keith, 122
chronological order, 40, 50
   for informational talks, 97
Cicero, 11
Cleese, John, 136
clip art, 170–171

clothing. *See* dress
colors
   background, 174–175, 176
   fill, 163
comfort, audience, 101, 107, 120–121
Common Cause, 29
comparison/contrast, 31
conversation, speeches as, 76
copyright issues, 137
Corel Draw, 147
corporate presentations outline, 154
cortisol, 10
cover transitions, 166
credentials, 103
credibility, 87, 90, 95, 181
   slides and, 134
criticism, constructive, 118–119
CRM Learning, 137
cues, 64–65
cuts, 166

D

Dale Carnegie system, 18, 155
Dialect Accent Specialists Inc., 76
diaphragm, 68
dress, 17, 88–89, 191
   levels of, 89
   for men, 91
   videoconferences and, 197
   for women, 90
dummy slides, 133

E

Einstein, Albert, 30
emotional appeals, 100–101
emphasis
   cues for in notes, 64–65
   vocal tone and, 70, 71
endings, 186
   after Q&A sessions, 56–57, 194–195
   closing statements, 195
   outlining, 43
   writing, 54–55

energy, 81

English as a Second Language (ESL), 76

Enterprise Media LLC, 137

entrances, making, 80–81

equipment
    determining available, 16–17
    failures of, 147
    slide, 135
    video, 136–137

evaluation forms, 109

expectations, audience, 116–117

expertise
    communicating without boasting, 15
    feeling unqualified and, 18
    how to demonstrate, 15

extemporaneous speaking, 58, 77

eye contact, 13, 84–85
    avoiding, 91
    checking notes and, 19
    definition of, 79
    glasses and, 90
    nervousness and, 91
    in Q&A sessions, 57
    reading speeches and, 85

F

facial expressions, 193

facts, 24–25, 184–185
    conveying interestingly, 34
    opening with, 49
    sources for, 33

fades, 166

fear, 6–19
    calming, 12–13
    concealing, 86–87
    controlling, 192, 196
    as evolutionary response, 10–11
    preparation to counteract, 14–15
    of public speaking, 11
    questions to answer to avoid, 16–17

feedback
    test audience, 118–119, 190
    videoconferences and, 197

Fields, Debbi, 28

fight or flight, 8, 10–11

fill colors, 163

first impressions, 80–81, 86

Fitzgerald, Suzanne, 59, 91, 197

Fletcher, Leon, 19

flip charts, 140–141, 145

flow, 52

focus, 12–13
    narrowing, 22–23

fonts, 158, 160, 174, 189

format, 39

G

Gardner, John, 29

gestures, 193. *See also* body language
    inappropriate, 73

glasses, 90

Gleeck, Fred, 111

Gold Disk Astound, 147

graphics, selecting, 175, 189

gratitude, expressing, 34, 81

H

handouts, 142–143, 189
    in PowerPoint, 172–173
    pros and cons of, 145
    for seminars, 109

Harper's Magazine, 33

heckling, 125

height, 18

hierarchy of needs, 100–101

historical references, opening with, 49

hoarseness, 67

humor, 26–27
    appropriateness of, 117
    concerns about, 34
    effective use of, 124
    improving presentations with, 30–31
    opening with, 49
    panels and, 105
    sources for, 35
    videotapes and, 136

I

IBM, 88
inflection, 70, 71
  upward, 72
informational talks, 94–95, 96–97
interviews, 197
introductions
  credibility and, 90
  knowing who will perform, 17
  protocol of, 102–103
  sample, 103
  writing your own, 80–81
"I" statements, 119

J

jargon, 39
Jeary, Tony, 19
Jessel, George, 11
jewelry, 191
Johnson, Spencer, 136
jokes, opening with, 49. *See also* humor
Jones, James Earl, 70
judgments, 119

K

Karaski, Paul, 111
key points, 50–51
  build slides for, 168–169
  cues for emphasis of, 64–65
  number of, 51
  summarizing, 54
  writing, 51
Kwakiutl Indians, 25

L

layoffs, 101
layouts, 160
leadership, 181
  humor in, 26–27
Lincoln, Abraham, 29
logo slides, 133
Lotus Freelance, 147
Lowe, Doug, 177

M

MacManus, Judith A., 77
Maselli, Frank, 111
Maslow, Abraham, 100–101
McKay Training Videos, 137
memories, negative, 11
memorization, 58
metaphors, 34
microphones, using, 67, 120, 193
Microsoft Office Professional/Premium,
  151
Microsoft PowerPoint. *See* PowerPoint
Mira, Thomas, 59, 91, 197
mission statements, 21–23
  limitations of, 34
  multiple, 51
  outlining, 42
  sample, 23
  type of talk and, 95
  writing, 38–39
mistakes, dealing with, 19
moderators, 106–107, 111
mood setting, 48–49
motion pictures, 137. *See also* videotapes
motivational talks, 94–95, 100–101
mumbling, 72, 76
Murrow, Edward R., 11

N

nasal voice, 73
National Public Radio, 32
nervousness. *See* fear
nervous tics, 73
Newman, Edwin, 11
Newsweek, 32
Nexis/Lexis, 184
notes
  cues in for emphasis, 64–65
  eye contact and, 19
  pointers on creating, 63
  in PowerPoint, 162, 172–173
  vs. writing out speeches, 62–63
notes of appreciation, 109

O

observations, 119
openings, 186
  getting ideas for, 58
  options for, 49
  outlining, 42
  writing, 48–49
organizational patterns, 40–41
organization charts, 162
outlines, writing, 38–39, 42–43
  in PowerPoint, 152–155, 172–173
overhead transparencies, 138–139
  pros and cons of, 145

P

panels, 15, 93
  moderating, 106–107, 111
  participating in, 104–105
  Q&A in, 107
panes, PowerPoint, 156–157
participant packets, 109
pauses, 37, 46
  power of, 69
Pearl, Minnie, 70
personal style, 86–87
persuasive talks, 94–95, 98–99
  judging success of, 110
pitch, 70, 73
podiums, 120–121
pointers, 147
PowerPoint, 134–135, 147, 148–177
  acquiring, 151
  adding/deleting slides in, 159
  AutoContent Wizard, 152–155
  background colors in, 176
  background textures, 163
  blank presentations in, 170–171
  build slides, 168–169
  chart editor, 163
  chart library, 151
  clip art, 170–171
  color choices in, 176
  editing in, 158–159
  fill colors in, 163
  making notes in, 162
  merging presentations in, 176
  Organization Chart feature, 162
  outlines in, 152–155
  printing/presenting presentations in, 172–173
  pros and cons of, 144
  room size and, 135
  saving presentations in, 158
  selecting/using slides in, 174–175
  slide views, 164–165
  spell checking, 177
  templates, 160–161
  text in, 174–175, 176, 177
  transitions, 166–167
  vocabulary in, 156–157
  what it is, 150–151
practice, 74–75, 190
  eye contact and, 85
  test audiences for, 118–119
  preparation of anecdotes, statistics, facts, 24–25
  to be a panelist, 105
  fear avoidance through, 14–15
  of humor, 26–27
  purpose of the talk in, 22–23
  time line for, 182–183
  vs. extemporaneous speaking, 58
  when to begin, 19
presence, 86–87
presentations
  being asked to give, 180–181
  benefits of giving, 9, 181
  breathing and, 68–69
  entrances in, 80–81
  five days before, 188–189
  format for, 38–39
  improving, 30–31
  knowing other presenters of, 16
  maintaining control of, 141
  morning of, 191
  notes for, 64–65

one day before, 190
one week before, 186–187
reading, 62–63
rehearsing, 74–75
speaking voice in, 66–67, 70–73
ten days before, 184–185
ten minutes before, 192
two weeks before, 182–183
types of, 92–111
writing, 36–59
presentation software, 132–133, 134–135, 147
handouts from, 143
PowerPoint, 148–177
pros and cons of, 144
problem/solution order, 40, 50
projectors
overhead, 138–139
practice with, 133
videotape, 136–137
project presentation outline, 155
proofreading, 188–189
proposition of fact, 99
proposition of policy, 99
proposition of value, 99
props, 145
purpose, mission statements for, 21–23

Q

question and answer sessions, 56–57, 194
beginning, 55
ending, 194
outlining, 43
with panels, 107
understandability and, 59
questions
checklist of preparation, 182–183
direct, 49
engaging the audience with, 14–15
rhetorical, 49
quotations, 27, 28–29
energizing presentations with, 31
opening with, 49
sources for, 32–33

R

Reader's Digest, 32
reading presentations, 62–63
eye contact and, 85
refreshments, 120–121
rehearsal, 74–75, 190
test audiences for, 118–119
research
fact gathering in, 184–185
fear avoidance and, 14–15
on humor, 26–27
on voice, 66
Web sites for, 185
Revere, Paul, 25
revisions, 53
room setup, 16
audience comfort and, 101, 107, 120–121
light levels, 146
rehearsals in, 75
visual aids and, 130–131
working with, 130–131
Rozakis, Laurie, 19
Rutledge, Patrice-Anne, 177

S

sales/marketing presentation outline, 155
scanned images, 175
scheduling issues, 108–109
scripted speeches, 62–63
visual aid cues in, 129
Seinfeld, Jerry, 7, 11
seminars, leading, 108–109
sentence length, 37, 46
sight lines, 120–121
silence, power of, 69
similes, 34
slide mounts, 133
slides. *See also* PowerPoint
color in, 174–175, 176
definition of in PowerPoint, 156
light levels and, 146
35mm, 132–133, 135, 144, 150
power of, 129

from presentation software, 134–135, 144

pros and cons of, 144

text and, 188–189

tips for using, 174–175

sound systems, 120–121

spatial order, 40

for informational talks, 97

speech coaches, 12–13, 76

speech faults, fixing, 72–73

speech therapists, 76

speech types, 94–95

spell checking, 177, 188–189

stage setting, 120–121

Stanford University, 26

statistics, 24–25

energizing, 30

interpreting, 25

sources for, 33

Stone, Janet, 77

stories, 30–31

success, visualizing, 180–181

summaries, 186

T

teamwork, facts about, 33

teleconferences, 197

television appearances, 197

temperature, room, 120–121

Templeton, Melody, 59, 91, 197

Temple University, 26–27

test audiences, 118–119

themes, determining in advance, 16

3M Corporation, 129

timing

controlling fear and, 13

determining available time and, 17

including all the material and, 59

stretching, 51

title slides, 133

tone, 70

Toogood, Granville N., 77

topical order, 40

for informational talks, 97

transitions, 37

outlining, 42

PowerPoint, 166–167

writing, 52, 186

Twain, Mark, 77

typefaces, 158, 160, 174, 189

U

U.C.L.A., 66

uncover transitions, 166

uppercase letters, 189

V

verbs, active, 37, 46

videotapes, 136–137

pros and cons of, 144

visual aids, 74, 126–147

flip charts, 140–141

handouts, 142–143

overhead transparencies, 138–139

power of, 128–129

pros and cons of, 144–145

selecting, 130–131, 144–145

setting the scene for, 130–131

slides, 132–135

videotape, 136–137

visualization, 180–181, 192, 196

voice, 66–67, 193

accents, 76

characteristics of, 70

exercises for, 71

food and, 191

nasal, 73

soft, 110

speech faults and, 72–73

W

Watson, T. J., Sr., 88

Web sites

Altavista.com, 185

desktoppub.about.com/cs/power point/, 177

desktoppub.about.com/cs/power
    pointadv/, 177
Findarticles.com, 185
Gallup.com, 185
Google.com, 185
Loc.gov, 185
Nationalgeographic.com, 185
Newsdirectory.com, 185
Nytimes.com, 185
Webcrawler.com, 185
www.About.com, 135
www.adobe.com/products/photoshop/
    main.html, 147
www.bartleby.com, 33, 185
www.breathing.com, 77
www.creatingvoices.com, 77
www.crmfilms.com, 137
www.dalecarnegie.com, 18
www.deepsloweasy.com, 77
www.demographics.com, 33, 185
www.dialectaccentspecialists.com, 76
www.dogpile.com, 35, 185
www.ee.ed.ac.uk/~gerard/
    Management/art1.html, 19
www.encarta.com, 33
www.enterprisemedia.com, 137
www.executive-speaker.com, 91
www.harpers.org, 33, 185
www.idea-bank.com, 32, 185
www.infoplease.com, 33
www.mckaytrainingvideos.com, 137
www.microsoft.com/office/power
    point, 147, 177
www.msnbc.com/news/
    NW-front_Front.asp, 32
www.notmuch.com, 35
www.npr.org, 33, 185
www.pbs.org/greatspeeches, 35
www.personal.psu.edu/users/s/b/sbw3/
    workbook, 19
www.presentations.com, 91
www.rd.com, 32, 185
www.rhymezone.net, 35

www.salon.com, 35, 185
www.temple.edu/speech, 19
www.ukans.edu/cwis/units/coms2/
    vpa/vpa.htm, 19
www.voicecoach.net, 77
www.wesleyan.edu/librt/tutlist. htm, 19
Western Union, 28
Westheimer, Ruth, 18
Wilder, Lilyan, 19
wipes, 166
word choice
    active voice, 52, 187
    big words, 41, 52
    jargon, 39
    samples of, 47
    for speaking vs. writing, 46–47
    verbs, 37
wrap-ups, 54–55, 186
    after Q&A sessions, 56–57
    outlining, 43
writing, 36–59, 186–187
    body of the talk, 50–51
    drafts, 187
    for the ear, 46–47
    endings, 54–55
    flow in, 52
    handwriting, 196
    introductions, 80–81
    openings, 48–49
    organization for, 40–41
    outlines, 38–39, 42–43
    revisions, 53
    sample of, 44–45

THE AUTHOR: UP CLOSE

Jude Westerfield has worked in corporate communications for over 20 years. She has written speeches for executives in the high-tech, financial services, and healthcare industries, as well as coached them on how best to give their presentations. Her essays and prose have appeared in *The New York Times* and various Internet and trade publications. She lives in Westchester County, New York.

Barbara J. Morgan Publisher, Silver Lining Books

Barnes & Noble Basics™

Barb Chintz Editorial Director

Leonard Vigliarolo Design Director

Barnes & Noble Basics™ *Giving a Presentation*

Anne Marie O'Connor Design Assistant

Alison Corrie Design Assistant

Ann Stewart Picture Research

Emily Seese Editorial Assistant

Della R. Mancuso Production Manager